WHEN BUFFALO RAN

PEOPLE LOOKING FROM THE LODGES

WHEN BUFFALO RAN

BY GEORGE BIRD GRINNELL

NORMAN : UNIVERSITY OF OKLAHOMA PRESS

149572

Table of Contents.

List of Illustrations.

Publisher's Note

THE TIME of which George Bird Grinnell writes in the opening lines of his book was about 1850. No white observer of his era (he was born in 1849 and died in 1938) knew more intimately the life and ways of the Plains Indian tribes, or for so long a period. Grinnell went on the Custer expedition to the Black Hills in 1874, and as ethnologist, historian, and writer spent much time thereafter with the tribe that was clearly his favorite, the Cheyennes, but he also worked with the Blackfeet, Pawnees, and others. From 1889, when his first book, *Pawnee Hero Stories and Folk Tales,* appeared, he wrote thirteen books of serious intent, of which *The Fighting Cheyennes* (1915) and *The Cheyenne Indians* (1923) are best known.

The boy Wikis and his people are not identified by Grinnell in his account, but the internal evidence is that they were Northern Cheyennes, living close to and allied with the Arapahoes, and in conflict with the Blackfeet and Utes. We can readily accept the author's statement that "The incidents of this simple story are true," and we can justifiably believe that they were derived from one or more informants living the life so clearly and arrestingly described in these pages.

SAVOIE LOTTINVILLE
University of Oklahoma Press

The Plains Country.

SEVENTY years ago, when some of the events here re-
counted took place, Indians were Indians, and the plains
were the plains indeed.

Those plains stretched out in limitless rolling swells
of prairie until they met the blue sky that on every hand
bent down to touch them. In spring brightly green, and
spangled with wild flowers, by midsummer this prairie
had grown sere and yellow. Clumps of dark green cottonwoods marked the courses of the infrequent streams
—for most of the year the only note of color in the land-
scape, except the brilliant sky. On the wide, level river
bottoms, sheltered by the enclosing hills, the Indians
pitched their conical skin lodges and lived their simple
lives. If the camp were large the lodges stood in a wide
circle, but if only a few families were together, they were
scattered along the stream.

In the spring and early summer the rivers, swollen by
the melting snows, were often deep and rapid, but a little
later they shrank to a few narrow trickles running over
a bed of sand, and sometimes the water sank wholly out
of sight.

The animals of the prairie and the roots and berries
that grew in the bottoms and on the uplands gave the
people their chief sustenance.

In such surroundings the boy Wikis was born and

grew up. The people that he knew well were those of his own camp. Once a year perhaps, for a few weeks, he saw the larger population of a great camp, but for the most part half a dozen families of the tribe, with the buffalo, the deer, the wolves, and the smaller animals and birds, were the companions with whom he lived and from whom he learned life's lessons.

The incidents of this simple story are true.

The life of those days and the teachings received by the boy or the girl who was to take part in it have passed away and will not return.

The Attack on the Camp.

It is the first thing that I can recollect, and comes back to me now dimly—only as a dream. My mother used to tell me of it, and often to laugh at me. She said I was then about five or six years old.

I must have been playing with other little boys near the lodge, and the first thing that I remember is seeing people running to and fro, men jumping on their horses, and women gathering up their children. I remember how the men called to each other, and that some were shouting the war cry; and then that they all rode away in the same direction. My mother rushed out and caught me by the hand, and began to pull me toward the lodge, and then she stopped and in a shrill, sweet voice began to sing; and other women that were running about stopped too, and began to sing songs to encourage their husbands and brothers and sons to fight bravely; for enemies were attacking the camp.

I did not understand it at all, but I was excited and glad to hear the noise, and to see people rushing about. Soon I could hear shooting at a distance. Then presently I saw the men come riding back toward the camp; and saw the enemy following them down toward the lodges, and that there were many of these strangers, while our people were only a few. But still my people kept stopping and turning and fighting. Now the noise was louder. The women sang their strong heart songs more shrilly, and I could hear more plainly the whoops of men, and the blowing of war whistles, and the reports of guns.

Presently one of our men fell off his horse. The enemy charged forward in a body to touch him, and our few men rushed to meet them, to keep them from striking the fallen one, and from taking the head. And now the women began to be frightened, and some of them ran away. My mother rushed to the lodge, caught up my little sister, and threw her on her back, and holding me by the hand, ran toward the river. By this time I was afraid, and I ran as hard as I could; but my legs were short and I could not keep up, even though my mother had a load on her back. Nevertheless, she pulled me along. Every little while I stumbled and lost my feet; but she dragged me on, and as she lifted me up, I caught my feet again, and ran on.

Before long I began to tire, and I remember that I wanted to stop. In after years mother used to laugh at me about this, and say that I had asked her to throw away my sister, and to put me on her back and carry me instead. She used to say, too, that if she had been obliged to throw away either child I should have been the one left behind, for as I was a boy, and would grow up to be a warrior, and to fight the enemies of our tribe, I might very likely be killed anyway, and it might as well be earlier as later.

When we reached the river, my mother threw herself

into it. Usually it was not more than knee-deep, but at this time the water was high from the spring floods, and my mother had to swim, holding my sister on her back, and at the same time supporting me, for though I could swim a little, I was not strong enough to breast the current, and without help would have been carried away.

After we had crossed the river and come out on the other side, we looked back toward the village, and could see that the enemy were retreating. They might easily have killed or driven off the few warriors of our small camp, but not far from us there was a larger camp of our people, and when they heard the shooting and the shouting, they came rushing to help us; and when the enemy saw them coming, they began to yield and then to run away. Our warriors followed and killed some of them; but the most of them got away after having killed four warriors of our camp, whose hard fighting and death had perhaps saved the little village.

After the enemy had retreated, my mother crossed the river again, being helped over by a man who was on the side opposite the camp, and who let us ride his horse, while he held its tail and swam behind it.

In the village that night there was mourning for those who had lost their lives to save their friends. Their relations cried very pitifully over the dead; and early the next day their bodies were carried to the top of a hill near the village, and buried there.

After the mourning for the dead was ended, the people had dances over the scalps that had been taken from the enemy, rejoicing over the victory. Men and women blackened their faces, and danced in a circle about the scalps, held on poles; and old men and old women shouted the names of those men who had been the bravest in the fight. We little boys looked on and sang and danced by ourselves away from the circle.

It was soon after this that my uncle made me a bow and some blunt-headed arrows, with which he told me I should hunt little birds, and should learn to kill food, to help support my mother and sisters, as a man ought to do. With these arrows I used to practice shooting, trying to see how far I could shoot, how near I could send the arrow to the mark I shot at; and afterwards, as I grew a little older, hunting in the brush along the river, or on the prairie not far from the camp with the other little boys. We hunted the blackbirds, or the larks, or the buffalo birds that fed among the horses' feet, or the other small birds that lived among the bushes and trees in the bottom. If I killed a little bird, as sometimes I did, my mother cooked it and we ate it.

This was a happy time for me. We little boys played together all the time. Sometimes the older boys allowed us to go with them, when they went far from the village, to hunt rabbits, and when they did this, sometimes they told us to carry back the rabbits that they had killed; and I remember that once I came back with the heads of three rabbits tucked under my belt, killed by my cousin, who was older than I. Then we used to go out and watch the men and older boys playing at sticks; and we had little sticks of our own, and our older brothers and cousins made us wheels; and we, too, played the stick game among ourselves, rolling the wheel and chasing it as hard as we could; but, for the most part, we threw our sticks at marks, trying to learn how to throw them well, and how to slide them far over the ground.

I remember another thing—a sad thing—that happened when I was a very little boy.

It was winter; the snow lay deep on the ground; a few lodges of people were camped in some timber among the foothills; buffalo were close, and game was plenty; the camp was living well. With the others I played about the camp, spinning tops on the ice, sliding down hill on a bit —of parfleche, or on a sled made of buffalo ribs, and sometimes hunting little birds in the brush. All this I know about from having heard my mother tell of it; it is not in my memory. This is what I remember: One day, with one of my friends, I had gone a little way from the camp, and down the stream. A few days before there had been a heavy fall of snow, and after that some warm days, so that the top of the snow had melted. Then had come a hard cold, which had frozen it, so that on the snow there was a crust over which we could easily run.

As we were playing we went around the point of a hill, and suddenly, close to us, saw a big bull. He seemed to have come from the other side of the river, and was plowing his way through the deep snow, which came halfway up to the top of his hump. When we saw the bull we were a little frightened; but as we watched him we saw that

15

he could hardly move, and that after he had made a jump or two he stood still for a long time, puffing and blowing, before he tried to go further. As we watched him he came to a low place in the prairie, and here he sank still deeper in the snow, so that part of his head was hidden, and only his hump showed above it. My friend said to me, "Let us go up to this bull, and shoot him with our arrows." We began to go toward him slowly, and he did not see us until we had come quite close to him, when he turned and tried to run; but the snow was so deep that he could not go at all; on each side it rose up, and rolled over, away from him, as the water is pushed away and swells out on either side before a duck that is swimming. My friend was very brave, and he said to me, "I am going to shoot that bull, and count a coup on him"; and he ran up close to the bull, and shot his blunt-headed arrow against him, and then turned off. The bull tried hard to go faster, but the snow was too deep; and when I saw that he could not move, I, too, ran up close to him, and shot my arrow at him, and the arrow bounded off and fell on the snow. Again my friend did this, and then I did it; and each time the bull was frightened and struggled to get away: but the last time my friend did it the bull had reached higher ground, where the snow was not so deep, and he had more freedom. My friend shot his arrow into him, and I was following not far behind, expecting to shoot mine; but when the bull felt the blow of the last arrow, he turned toward my friend and made a quick rush; the snow was less

HUNTING IN THE BRUSH ALONG THE RIVER

deep; he went faster; my little friend slipped, and the bull caught him with his horns and threw him far. My friend fell close to me, and where he fell the snow was red with his blood, for the great horn had caught him just above the waist, and had ripped his body open nearly to the throat.

I went up to him in a moment, and, catching him, pulled him over the smooth crust, far from the bull; but when I stopped and looked at him, he was still, his eyes were dull, and he did not breathe; he was dead.

I did not know what to do. I had lost my friend, and I cried hard. Also, I wished to be revenged on the bull for what he had done; but I did not wish to be killed. I covered my friend with my robe, and started running fast to the camp, where I told my mother what had happened. Soon all the men in the camp, and some of the women, had started with me, back to where the bull was. My friend's relations were wailing and mourning, as they came along, and soon we reached his body, and his relations carried him back to the camp. Two of the men went to where the bull stood in the snow and killed him; and after he was dead I struck him with my bow.

Standing Alone.

ALWAYS as winter drew near, the camps came closer together, and the people began to make ready to start off on the hunt for buffalo. By this time food was scarce, and the people needed new robes; and now that the cold weather was at hand, the hair of the buffalo was long and shaggy, so that the robes would be soft and warm, to keep out the winter cold.

I remember that before the tribe started there used to be a great ceremony, but I was too young to understand what it all meant, though with the others I watched what the old men did, and wondered at it, for it seemed very solemn. There was a big circle about which the people stood or sat, and in the middle of the circle there were buffalo heads on the ground, and before them stood old men, who prayed and offered sacrifices, and passed their weapons and their sacred implements over the skulls, and then people danced; and not long after this the women loaded their lodges and their baggage on the horses, and put their little children into the cages on the travois, or piled them on the loaded pack horses; and then presently, in a long line, the village started off over the prairie, to look for buffalo.

Most of the way I walked or ran, playing with the other little boys, or looking through the ravines to try and find small birds, or a rabbit, or a prairie chicken.

Sometimes I rode a colt, too young yet to carry a load, or to be ridden by an older person, yet gentle enough to carry me. In this way I learned to ride.

When buffalo were found, the young men killed them, and then the whole camp, women and children, went out to where the buffalo lay, and meat and hides were brought in to the camp, where the women made robes, and dried meat. Food was plenty, and everybody was glad.

My grandmother lived in our lodge. She was an old woman with gray hair, and was always working hard. Whenever there were skins in the lodge she worked at them until they were tanned and ready for use. Often she used to talk to me, telling me about the old times; how our tribe used to fight with its enemies, and conquer them, and kill them; and how brave the men always were. She used to tell me that of all things that a man could do, the best thing was to be brave. She would say to me: "Your father was a brave man, killed by his enemies when he was fighting. Your grandfather, too, was brave, and counted many coups; he was a chief, and is looked up to by everyone. Your other grandfather was killed in a battle when he was a young man. The people that you have for relations have never been afraid, and you must not be afraid either. You must always do your best, because you have many relations who have been braves, and chiefs. You have no father to tell you how you ought to live, so now your other relations must try to help you as much as they can, and advise you what to do."

MY GRANDMOTHER LIVED IN OUR LODGE

Standing Alone.

She used to tell me of the ancient times, and of things that happened then, of persons who had strong spiritual power, and did wonderful things, and of certain bad persons and animals, who harmed people, and of the old times before the people had bows, when they did not kill animals for food, but lived on roots and berries. She told me that I must remember all these things, and keep them in my mind.

Sometimes my grandmother had hard pains in her legs, and it hurt her to walk, and when she had these pains she could not go about much, and could not work. When this happened, sometimes she used to ask me to go down to the stream and fetch her a skin of water; and I would whine, and say to her, "Grandmother, I do not want to carry water; men do not carry water." Then she would tell us some story about the bad things that had happened to boys who refused to carry water for their grandmothers; and when I was little these stories frightened me, and I would go for the water. So perhaps I helped her a little in some things after she was old. Yet she lived until I was a grown man; and so long as she lived she worked hard; except when she had these pains.

Sometimes my mother and some of her relations would go off and camp together for a long time; and then perhaps they would join a larger camp, and stay with them for a while. In these larger camps we children had much fun, playing our different games. We had many of these. Some, like those I have spoken of, we played in winter, and some we played in summer. Often the little girls caught some of the dogs, and harnessed them to little travois, and took their baby brothers and sisters, and others of the younger children, and moved off a little way from the camp, and there pitched their little lodges. The boys went too, and we all played at living in camp. In these camps we did the things that older people do. A boy and girl pretended to be husband and wife, and lived in the lodge; the girl cooked and the boy went out hunting. Sometimes some of the boys pretended that they were buffalo, and showed themselves on the prairie a little way off, and other boys were hunters, and went out to chase the buffalo. We were too little to have horses, but the boys rode sticks, which they held between their legs, and lashed with their quirts to make them go faster.

Among those who played in this way was a girl smaller than I, the daughter of Two Bulls—a brave man, a friend to my uncle. The little girl's name was Standing Alone; she was pretty and nice, and always pleasant; but she was always busy about something—always working hard, and when she and I played at being husband and wife, she was always going for wood, or pretending to dress hides. I liked her, and she liked me, and in these play camps we always had our little lodge together; but if I sat in the lodge, and pretended to be resting longer than she thought right, she used to scold me, and tell me to go out and hunt for food, saying that no lazy man could be her husband. When she said this I did not answer and seemed to pay no attention to her words, but sat for a little while, thinking, and then I went out of the

22

lodge, and did as she said. When I came in again, whether I brought anything or not, she was always pleasant.

Once, when we were running buffalo, one of the boys, who was a buffalo, charged me when I got near him, and struck me with the thorn which he carried on the end of his stick, and which we used to call the buffalo's horn. The thorn pierced me in the body, and, according to the law of our play, I was so badly wounded that I was obliged to die. I went a little way toward the village, and then pretended to be very weak. Then my companions carried me into the camp, and to the lodge, and Standing Alone mourned over her husband who had been killed while hunting buffalo. Then one of the boys, who pretended that he was a medicine man, built a sweat lodge, and doctored me, and I recovered.

The Way to Live.

I MUST have been ten years old when my uncle first began to talk to me. Long before this, when he had made a bow and some arrows for me, he had told me that I must learn to hunt, so that in the time to come I would be able to kill food, and to support my mother and sisters. "We must all eat," he had said, "and the Creator has given us buffalo to support life. It is the part of a man to kill food for the lodge, and after it has been killed, the women bring in the meat, and prepare it to be eaten, while they dress the hides for robes and lodge skins."

My uncle was a brave man, and was always going off on the warpath, searching for the camps of enemies, taking their horses, and sometimes fighting bravely. He was still a young man, not married; but was quiet and of good sense and all the people respected him. Even the chiefs and older men used to listen to him when he spoke; and sometimes he was asked to a feast to which many older men were invited.

All my life I have tried to remember what he told me this first time that he talked with me, for it was good advice, and came to me from a good man, who afterwards became one of the chiefs of the tribe.

One day, soon after he had returned from one of his warpaths, he said to me, early in the morning: "My son, get your bow and arrows, and you and I will go over into the hills, hunting. We will try to kill some rabbits, and perhaps we may find a deer."

I was glad to go with my uncle; no grown man had ever before asked me to go with him, and to have him speak to me like this made me feel glad and proud. I ran quickly and got my bow, and we set out, walking over the prairie. We walked a long way, and I was beginning to get tired, when we came to a place where we started first one rabbit and then another, and then a third. I shot at one, but missed it; and my uncle killed all three. After this we went up to the top of a high hill, to look over the country. We saw nothing, but as we sat there my uncle spoke to me, telling me of the things that he had done not long before; and after a time he began to tell me how I ought to live, and what I ought to do as I grew older.

He said to me: "My son, I am going to tell you some things that will be useful to you; and if you listen to what I say, your life will be easier for you to live; you will not make mistakes, and you will come to be liked and respected by all the people. Before many years now you will be a man, and as you grow up you must try more and more to do the things that men do. There are a few things that a boy must always remember.

"When older people speak to you, you must stop what you are doing and listen to what they say, and must do as they tell you. If anyone says to you, 'My son, go out and drive in my horses,' you must go at once; do not wait; do not make anyone speak to you a second time; start at once.

26

The Way to Live.

"You must get up early in the morning; do not let the sun, when it first shines, find you in bed. Get up at the first dawn of day, and go early out into the hills and look for your horses. These horses will soon be put in your charge, and you must watch over them, and must never lose them; and you must always see that they have water.

"You must take good care of your arms. Always keep them in good order. A man who has poor arms cannot fight.

"It is important for you to do all these things. But there is one thing more important than anything else, and that is to be brave. Soon you will be going on a warpath, and then you must strive always to be in the front of the fighting, and to try hard to strike many of the enemy. You must be saying all the time to yourself, 'I will be brave; I will not fear anything.' If you do that, the people will all know of it, and will look on you as a man.

"There is another thing: if by chance you should do anything that is great, you must not talk of it; you must never go about telling of the great things that you have done, or that you intend to do. To do that is not manly. When you are at war you may do brave things, and other people will see what you have done, and will tell of it. If you should chance to perform any brave act, do not speak of it; let your comrades do this; it is not for you to tell of the things that you have done.

"If you listen to my words you will become a good man, and will amount to something. If you let the wind blow them away, you will become lazy, and will never do anything."

So my uncle talked to me for a long time, and just as he had finished his talking, we saw, down in the valley below us, a deer come out from behind some brush, and feed for a little while, and then it went back into another patch of brush, and did not come out again.

"Ah," said my uncle, "I think we can kill that deer." We went around a long distance, to come down without being seen to where the deer was, and we had crept up close to the edge of the bushes before the deer knew that we were there. When we reached the place we walked around it, he on one side and I on the other; and presently the deer sprang up out of the bushes, and my uncle shot it with his arrow; and after it had run a distance it fell down, and when we got to it, was dead. I also shot at it with one of my sharp-pointed arrows, but I did not hit it. After we had cut up the meat of the deer, and made it into a pack, done up in the hide, we started back to the camp. I felt proud to have gone on a hunt with a man and to be carrying the rabbits.

As we walked along to the camp that night, my uncle told me other things. He said: "Always be careful to do nothing bad in camp. Do not quarrel and fight with your fellows. Men do not fight with each other in the camp; to do that is not manly."

You see, my uncle thought that I was now old enough to be taught some of the things a man ought to do, and he tried to help me; for my father was dead, and I had no

MY GRANDFATHER . . . LONG BEFORE HAD GIVEN UP THE WARPATH

one else to teach me. The words he spoke were all good words, and I have tried always to remember them.

The white people gather up their children and send them all to one place to be taught; but that is not the way we Indians do. Nevertheless, we try to teach our children in our way; for children must be taught, or they will not know anything, and if they do not know anything they will have no sense, and if they have no sense they will not know how to act.

When our children are small, the mother tries to keep them from making a noise. It is not fitting that young children should disturb older people. I am telling you about the way I was taught in the old times, when there were but few white people in the country.

Because we have no schools, like the white people, we have to teach our children by telling them what to do; it is only in this way that they can learn. They have lived but a short time, and cannot know much. We older ones, after we have lived many years, and have listened to what our fathers and brothers have taught us, know a good many things; but little children know nothing. We want them to be wise, so that they may live well with their people. But we want them to be wise also, so that when they are the chiefs and braves of the tribe they may rule the people well. We remember that before very long we ourselves shall no longer be here; and then the ones who are caring for the people's welfare will be these children that now are playing about the camps. Their relations, therefore, talk to the children, for they want their lives to be made easier for them; and they want also to have the next generation of people wise enough to help all the people to live. The men must hunt and go to war; the women must be good women, not foolish ones, and must be ready to work, and glad to take care of their husbands and their children. This is one of the reasons why we like to have them play at moving the camp, harnessing the old dogs to the travois, pitching the lodges, making clothing for the dolls; while the boys play at hunting buffalo and at making war journeys against their enemies. All are trying to learn how to live the life that our people have always lived.

My grandfather was an old man, who long before this had given up the warpath. He spent most of his time in the camp, and he used to make speeches to the little and big boys, and give them much good advice. Once I heard him talk to a group of boys playing near the lodge, and this is what he said: "Listen, you boys; it is time you did something. You sit here all day in the sun, and throw your arrows, and talk about things of the camp, but why do you not do something? When I was a boy it was not like this; then we were always trying to steal off and follow a war party. Some of those who did so were too little to fight; but we used to follow along, and try to help. In this way, even though we did nothing, we learned the ways of warriors. I do not want you boys to be lazy. It is not a lazy man who does great things, so that he is talked about in the camp, and his name is called aloud by all the people, when the war party returns."

Lessons of the Prairie.

ONCE when I was a little older, I was out on the hills one day, watching the horses. They were feeding quietly, and I lay on a hill and went to sleep. Suddenly I was awakened by a terrible crash close to my head, and I knew that a gun had been fired close to me, and I thought that the enemy had attacked me and were killing me, and would drive off the horses. I was badly frightened. I sprang to my feet, and started to run to my horse, and in doing this I ran away from the camp, but before I reached the horse I heard someone laughing, and when I looked around my uncle sat there on the ground, with the smoke still coming from his gun. He signed to me to come to him and sit down, and when I had done so, he said:

"My son, you keep a careless watch. You do not act as a man ought to do. Instead of sitting here looking over the prairie in all directions to see if enemies are approaching, or if there are any signs of strange people being near, you lie here and sleep. I crept up to you and fired my gun, to see what you would do. You did not stop to see where the noise came from, nor did you look about to see if enemies were here. You thought only of saving your body, and started to run away. This is not good. A warrior does not act like this; he is always watching all about him, to see what is going to happen, and if he is attacked suddenly, he tries to fight, or, if he cannot fight, he thinks more of giving warning to the people than he does of saving himself."

When my uncle spoke to me like this he made me feel bad, for of all people he was the one whom I most wished to please, and with him I wished to stand well. I considered a little before I said to him: "I was trying to run to my horse, and if I had got him I think I should have tried to reach the camp, and perhaps I should have tried to drive in some of the horses; but I was badly frightened, for I had been asleep and did not know what had happened."

"I think you speak truly," said my uncle, "but you should not have gone to sleep when you were sent out here to watch the horses. Boys who go to sleep when they ought to be looking over the country, and watching their horses, or men who get tired and go to sleep when they are on the warpath, never do much. I should like to have you always alert and watchful."

I made up my mind that I would hold fast to the words which my uncle spoke to me, and after this would not sleep when I was on herd.

It was not long after this that my uncle again told me to get my arrows, and come and hunt with him. He told me also to take my robe with me, and that we would go far up the river and be gone one night. I was glad to go, and we started.

All through the day we traveled up stream, going in low places, and traveling cautiously; for, although we were close to the camp, still my uncle told me no one could be sure that enemies might not be about, and that we might not be attacked at any time; so we went carefully. If we had to cross a hill, we crept up to the top of it, and lifted our heads up little by little, and looked over all the country, to see whether people were in sight; or game; or to see what the animals might be doing.

Once, when we stopped to rest, my uncle said to me: "Little son, this is one of the things you must learn; as you travel over the country, always go carefully, for you do not know that behind the next hill there may not be some enemy watching, looking over the country to see if someone may not be about. Therefore, it is well for you always to keep out of sight as much as you can. If you have to go to the top of the hill, because you wish to see the country, creep carefully up some ravine, and show yourself as little as possible. If you have to cross a wide flat, cover yourself with your robe, and stoop over, walking slowly, so that anyone far off may perhaps think it is a buffalo that he sees. In this respect the Indians are different from the white people; they are foolish, and when they travel they go on the ridges between the streams, because the road is level, and the going easy. But when they travel in this way everyone can see them from a long way off, and can hide in the path, and when they approach can shoot at them and kill them. The white people think that because they cannot see Indians, there are none about; and this belief has caused many white people to be killed."

When Buffalo Ran.

As I walked behind my uncle, following him over the prairie, I tried to watch him, and to imitate everything that he did. If he stopped, I stopped; if he bent down his head, and went stooping for a little way, I also stooped, and followed him; when he got down to creep, I, too, crept, so as to be out of sight.

That day, as the sun fell toward the west, my uncle went down to the river, and looked along the bank and the mud-bars, trying to learn whether any animals had been to the water; and when he saw tracks he pointed them out to me. "This," he said, "is the track of a deer. You see that it has been going slowly. It is feeding, because it does not go straight ahead, but goes now in one direction, and then in another, and back a little, not seeming to have any purpose in its wandering about, and here," showing me a place where a plant had been bitten off, "is where it was eating. If we follow along, soon we will see its tracks in the mud by the river." It was as he had said, and soon, in a little sand-bar, we saw the place where the animal had stopped. "You see," he said, "this was a big deer; here are his tracks; here he stopped at the edge of the water to drink; and then he went on across the river, for there are no tracks leading back to the bank. You will notice that he was walking; he was not frightened; he did not see nor smell any enemies."

Further up the river, on a sand-bar, he showed me the tracks of antelope, where the old ones had walked along quietly, and other smaller tracks, where the sand had

34

been thrown up; and these marks, he said, were made by the little kids, which were playing and running.

"Notice carefully," he said, "the tracks that you see, so that you will remember them, and will know them again. The tracks made by the different animals are not all alike. The antelope's hoof is sharp-pointed in front. Notice, too, that when his foot sinks in the mud there is no mark behind his footprint; while behind the footprint of a deer there are two marks, in soft ground, made by the little hoofs that the deer has on his foot."

We kept on further up the river, and when night came we stopped, and sat down in some bushes. All day long we had seen nothing that we could kill; but from a fold in his robe my uncle drew some dried meat, and we built a little fire of dried willow brush, that would make no smoke, and over this we roasted our meat, and ate; and my uncle talked to me again, saying: "My son, I like to have you come out with me, and travel about over the country. You have no father to teach you, and I am glad to take you with me, and to tell you the things that I know. It is a good thing to be a member of our tribe, and it is a good thing to belong to a good family in that tribe. You must always remember that you come of good people. Your father was a brave man, killed fighting bravely against the enemy. I want you to grow up to be a brave man and a good man. You must love your relations, and must do everything that you can for them. If the enemy should attack the village, do not run away; think always first of defending your own people. You have a mother, and sisters, who will depend on you for their living, and for their credit. They love you, and you must always try to do everything that you can for them. Try to learn about hunting, and to become a good hunter, so that you may support them. But, above all things, try to live bravely and well, so that people will speak well of you and your relations will be proud.

"You are only a boy now, but the time will come when you will be a man, and must act a man's part. Now your relations all respect you. They do not ask you to do woman's work; they treat you well. You have a good bed, and whenever you are hungry, food is given you. Do you know why it is that you are treated in this way? I will tell you. Your relations know that you are a man, and that you will grow up to go to war, and fight; perhaps often to be in great danger. They know that perhaps they may not have you long with them; that soon you may be killed. Perhaps even to-night or to-morrow, before we get back to the camp, we may be attacked, and may have to fight, and perhaps to die. It is for this cause that you are treated better than your sisters; because at any moment you may be taken away. This you should understand."

After we had eaten it began to grow dark, and pretty soon my uncle stood up and tied up his waist again, and we set out once more, going up the river. I wanted to ask my uncle where we were going, but I knew that he had some reason for moving away from the camp, and before I had spoken to him about it we had gone a mile or two, and it was quite dark, and we stopped again in another clump of bushes. Here we sat down, and my uncle said to me: "My son, here we will sleep. Where we stopped and ate, just before the sun set, was a good place to camp, but it may be that an enemy was watching from the top of some hill, and may have seen us go into those bushes. If he did, perhaps he will creep down there to-night, hoping to kill us; and if there were several persons they may go down there and surround those bushes. I did not want to stop there where we might have been seen, and so when it grew dark we came on here. We will sleep here, but will build no fire."

The next morning, before day broke, my uncle roused me, and we went to the top of a high hill not far off. We reached it before the sun rose, and lay on top of it, looking off over the prairie. From here we could see a long way. Many animals were in view, buffalo and antelope, and down in the river bottom a herd of elk. For a long time we lay there watching, but everywhere it was quiet. The animals were not moving; no smokes were seen in the air; birds were not flying to and fro, as if waiting for the hunter to kill a buffalo, or for people to fight and kill each other, when they might feed on the flesh.

After we had watched a long time, my uncle said: "I see no signs of people. Let us creep down this ravine, and get among the bushes, and perhaps we can kill one of these elk." We did as he had said; and before very long had come near to the elk. Then he told me to wait there. I stopped and for a few moments I could see him creeping up nearer and nearer to the elk. Presently they started and ran; and one cow turned off to cross the river, and as she was crossing it she fell in the water.

My uncle stood up and motioned to me to go down to where the elk lay. We met there and cut up the elk, and my uncle took a big load of meat on his back, and I a smaller load, and we started back toward the village.

As we were returning, he spoke to me again, saying: "I want you to remember that of all the advice I give you the chief thing is to be brave. If you start out with a war party, to attack enemies, do not be afraid. If your friends are about to make a charge on the enemy, still do not be afraid. Watch your friends, and see how they act, and try to do as the others do. Try always to have a good horse, and to be in the front of the fighting. To be brave is what makes a man. If you are lucky, and count a coup, or kill an enemy, people will look on you as a man. Do not fear anything. To be killed in battle is no disgrace. When you fight, try to kill. Ride up close to your enemy. Do not think that he is going to kill you; think that you are going to kill him. As you charge, you must be saying to yourself all the time, 'I will be brave; I will not fear anything.'

"In your life in the camp remember this too; you must always be truthful and honest with all your people. Never say anything that is not true; never tell a lie, even for a joke—to make people laugh. When you are in the company of older people, listen to what they say, and try to remember; thus you will learn. Do not say very much;

it is just as well to let other people talk while you listen. If you have a friend, cling close to him; and if need be, give your life for him. Think always of your friend before you think of yourself."

That night we reached the camp again. My uncle left the meat that he had killed at my mother's lodge.

On a Buffalo Horse.

I HAD lived twelve winters when I did something which made my mother and all my relations glad; for which they all praised me, and which first caused my name to be called aloud through the camp.

It was the fall of the year, and the leaves were dropping from the trees. Long ago the grass had grown yellow; and now sometimes when we awoke in the morning it was white with frost; little places in the river bottom, where water had stood in the springtime, and which were still wet, were frozen in the morning; and all the quiet waters had over them a thin skin of clear ice. Great flocks of water birds were passing overhead, flying to the south; and many of them stopped in the streams, resting and feeding. There were ducks of many sorts, and the larger geese, and the great white birds with black tips to their wings, and long yellow bills; and the cranes that fly over, far up in the sky, looking like spots, but whose loud callings are heard plainly as they pass along. Often we saw flocks of these walking on the prairie, feeding on the grasshoppers; and sometimes they all stopped feeding and stuck up their heads, and then began to dance together, almost as people dance.

We boys used to travel far up and down the bottom, trying to creep up to the edge of the bank, or to the puddles of water, where the different birds sat, to get close enough to kill them with our arrows. It was not easy to do this, for generally the birds saw us before we could get near enough; and then, often, even if we had the chance to shoot, we missed, and the birds flew away, and we had to wade out and get back our arrows.

One day I had gone with my friend a long way up the river, and we had tried several times to kill ducks, but had always missed them. We had come to a place where the point of a hill ran down close to the river, on our side, and as we rounded the point of this hill, suddenly we saw close before us three cranes, standing on the hillside; two of them were gray and further off, but one quite near to us was still red, by which we knew that it was a young one. I was ahead of my friend, and as soon as I saw the cranes I drew my arrow to its head, and shot at the young one, which spread its wings and flew a few yards, and then came down, lying on the hillside, with its wings stretched wide, for the arrow had passed through its body. I rushed upon it and seized it, while the old cranes flew away. Then I was glad, for this was the largest bird that I had ever killed; and you know that the crane is a wise bird, and people do not often kill one.

After my friend and I had talked about it, I picked up the bird and put it on my back, holding the neck in one hand, and letting the legs drag on the ground behind me; and so we returned to camp. When we reached the village some of the children saw us coming, and knew me, and ran ahead to my mother's lodge, and told her that her boy was coming, carrying a great bird; and she and my sisters came out of the lodge and looked at me. I must have looked strange, for the crane's wings were partly spread, and hung down on either side of me; and when I had nearly come to the lodge, my mother called out: "What is the great bird that is coming to our lodge? I am afraid of it," and then she and the children ran in the door. Then they came out again, and when I reached the lodge, all looked at the bird, and said how big it was, and how fine, and that it must be shown to my uncle before it was cooked. They sent word to him, asking him to come to the lodge, and soon he did so, and when he saw what I had killed, he was glad, and told me that I had done well, and that I was lucky to have killed a crane. "There are many grown men," said he, "who have never killed a crane; and you have done well. I wish to have this known."

He called out in a loud voice, and asked Bellowing Cow, a poor old woman, to come to the lodge and see what his son had done; and he sent one of the boys back to his lodge, telling him to bring a certain horse. Soon the boy returned, leading a pony; and when Bellowing Cow had come, my uncle handed her the rope that was about the pony's neck, and told her to look at this bird that his son had killed.

"We have had good luck," he said; "my son has killed this wise bird; he is going to be a good hunter, and will kill much meat. In the time to come, after he has grown to be a man, his lodge will never lack food. His women will always have plenty of robes to dress."

Then Bellowing Cow mounted her horse and rode around the village, singing a song, in which she told how lucky I had been; that I had killed a crane, a bird that many grown men had not killed; and that I was going to be a good hunter, and always fortunate in killing food. My uncle did not give the bird to Bellowing Cow; he kept it, and told my mother to cook it; and he said to her: "Save for me the wing bones of this bird, and give them to me, in order that I may make from them two war whistles, which my son may carry when he has grown old enough to go to war against his enemies."

I was proud of what had happened, and it made me feel big to listen to this poor old woman as she rode through the village singing her song.

What he did at this time showed some things about my uncle. It showed that he liked me; it showed that he was proud of what I had done; and it showed, too, that he was a person of good heart, since he called to see what I had done a poor old woman who had nothing, and gave her a horse. It would have been as easy for him to have called some chief or rich man who had plenty of horses, and then sometime this chief or rich man would have given him a horse for some favor done him.

I had killed the crane with a pointed arrow, of which I had three, though in my hunting for little birds I still used blunt arrows. My uncle had made me another bow, which was almost as large as a man's bow; and I was practicing with it always, trying to make my right arm strong, to bend it, so that it might send the arrow with full force.

The next summer, when the tribe had started off to look for buffalo, I spoke one night to my uncle, as he was sitting alone in his lodge, and said to him: "Father, is it not now time for me to try to kill buffalo? I am getting now to be a big boy, and I think big enough to hunt. I should like to have your opinion about this." For a time he sat smoking and considering, and then he said: "Son, I think it is time you should begin to hunt; you are now old enough to do some of the things that men do. I have watched you, and I have seen that you know how to use the bow. The next time that we run buffalo, you shall come with me, and we will see what we can do. You shall ride one of my buffalo horses, and you shall overtake the buffalo, and then we shall see whether you are strong enough to drive the arrow far into the animal."

It was not long after this that buffalo were found, and when the tribe went out to make the surround, my uncle told me to ride one of his horses, and to keep close to him. As we were going toward the place where the surround was to be made, he said to me: "Now, to-day we will try to catch calves, and you shall see whether you can kill one. You may remember this, that if you shoot an arrow into the calf, and blood begins to come from its mouth, it will soon die, you need not shoot at it again, but may go on to overtake another, and kill it. Then, perhaps, after a little while you can chase big buffalo. One thing you must remember. If you are running

45

buffalo, do not be afraid of them. Ride your horse close up to the buffalo, as close as you can, and then let fly the arrow with all your force. If the buffalo turns to fight, your horse will take you away from it; but, above all things, do not be afraid; you will not kill buffalo if you are afraid to get close to them."

We rode on, and before the surround was made we could see the yellow calves bunched up at one side of the herd. My uncle pointed them out to me, and said, "Now, when the herd starts, try to get among those calves, and remember all that I have told you."

At length the soldiers gave the word for the charge, and we all rushed toward the buffalo. They turned to run, and a great dust rose in the air. That day there were many men on fast horses, but my uncle's horse was faster than all; and because I was little and light, he ran through the big buffalo, and was soon close to the calves. When he was running through the buffalo I was frightened, for they seemed so big, and they crowded so on each other, and their horns rattled as they knocked together, as the herd parted and pushed away on either side, letting me pass through it.

In only a short time I was running close to a yellow calf. It ran very fast, and for a little while I could not overtake it; but then it seemed to go slower, and my horse drew up close to it. I shot an arrow and missed it, and then another, and did not miss; the arrow went deep into it, just before the short ribs, and a moment afterward I could see blood coming from the calf's mouth; and I ran on to get another. I did kill another, and then stopped and got down. The herd had passed, and I began to butcher the last calf; and before I had finished my uncle rode up to me and said, "Well, son, did you kill anything?" I told him that I had killed two calves; and we went back and looked for the other. He helped me to butcher, and we put the meat and skins of both calves on my horse and then returned to the camp.

When we reached there, my uncle stood in front of the lodge, and called out with a loud voice, saying: "This day my son has chased buffalo, and has killed two calves. I have given one of my best horses to Red Fox." This he called out several times, and at the same time he sent a young man to his lodge, telling him to bring a certain good horse, which he named. Before very long the young man came with the horse, and about the same time the old man Red Fox, who was poor and lame, and without relations, was seen limping toward the lodge, coughing as he came.

In his young days Red Fox had been a brave and had done many good things, but he had been shot in the thigh, in battle, and his leg had never healed, so that he could not go to war. After that, his wife and then his children one by one had died, or been killed in battle, and now he had nothing of his own, but lived in the lodge with friends—people who were kind to him. After Red Fox had mounted his horse, and had ridden off about the circle of the lodges, singing a song, in which he told what I had done, and how my uncle was proud of my success, and of how good his heart was toward poor people, so that when he made gifts he gave them to persons who had nothing, and not to people who were rich and happy, my uncle turned about and went into the lodge. He told the young man who had brought the horse to go out and call a number of his friends, and older people, to come that night to his lodge, to feast with him.

After they had come, and all had eaten, and while the pipe was being smoked, my uncle said: "Friends, I have called you to eat with me, because this day my son has killed two calves. He has done well, and I can see that he will be a good man. His lodge will not be poor for meat nor will his wife lack skins to tan, or hides for lodge skins. We have had good luck, and to-day my heart is glad; and it is for this reason that I have asked you to come and hear what my son has done, in order that you may be pleased, as I am pleased."

When he had finished speaking, Double Runner, an old man, whose hair was white, stood up on his feet and spoke, and said that I had done well. He spoke good words of my uncle because he had a kind heart and was generous, and liked to make people happy. He spoke also of my father, and said that it was bad for the tribe when the enemy killed him; but, nevertheless, he had died fighting, as a brave man would wish to die.

From that time on, so long as the buffalo were seen, I went out with the men of the camp. Sometimes I went alone, or with companions of my own age, and we tried to kill calves, but more than once I went with my uncle.

48

I KILLED MANY BUFFALO AND MY MOTHER DRESSED THE HIDES

On a Buffalo Horse.

The second time I rode with him he said to me that I had killed calves, and now I must try to kill big buffalo. I remembered what he had said about riding close to the buffalo, but I was afraid to do this, and yet I was ashamed to tell him that I was afraid. When the surround was made, my uncle and I were soon among the buffalo. I was riding my uncle's fast buffalo horse. My uncle rode on my right hand, and when we charged down and got among the buffalo we soon passed through the bulls and then drew up slowly on the cows, and those younger animals whose horns were yet straight. I thought we were going to pass on through these, and kill calves, but suddenly my uncle crowded his horse up close to me, and, pointing to a young bull, signed to me to shoot it. I did not want to, but my uncle kept crowding his horse more and more on me, and pushing me close to the bull. I was afraid of it; I thought that perhaps it would turn its head toward me and frighten my horse, and my horse could not get away because of my uncle's horse, and then my horse, and perhaps I, myself, would be killed; but there was not much time to think about it. I felt that I was not strong enough to kill a buffalo; I did not want to try; but all the time my uncle was signing to me, "Shoot, shoot." There was no way for me to escape, and I drew the arrow and shot into the buffalo. The point hit the animal between the ribs, and went in deep, yet not to the feathers. When I shot, my uncle sheered off, and I followed him; and in a moment, looking back, I saw that the blood was coming from the bull's nose and mouth; and then I knew that I had killed it. In a few moments it fell, and I went back to it. Then truly I thought that I had done something great, and I felt glad that I had killed a big buffalo. I forgot that a little while before I had been frightened, and had wanted to get away without shooting. I forgot that, except for my uncle, I should not have made this lucky shot. I felt as if I had done something, and something that was very smart and great. You see, I was only a boy.

This feeling did not last very long; after a little I remembered that except for my uncle I should have still been afraid of big buffalo, and should not have dared to go near enough to kill one, but should have been content to kill calves. My mind was still big for what I had done, and I felt thankful to my uncle for making me do it. I wanted to pass my hands over him—to express my gratitude to him—for all his kindness to me. No father could have done more for me than he had done, and always did.

That night when we came back to the camp my horse was carrying a great pile of meat; and when I stopped in front of the lodge, I called out to my mother to come and take my horse, and take the meat from it; for so my uncle had told me to do. "Now," he said, "you have become a man; you are able to hunt, and to kill food, and you must act as a man acts."

When my mother came out of the lodge she was astonished; she could hardly believe that it was I who had killed this buffalo. Nevertheless, she took the rope from me, and began to take the meat from the horse; and I went into the lodge and lay down on the bed by the fire to rest, for this too was what my uncle had told me to do.

The next time the camp made a surround, I rode alone, and this time I did not do so well. It is true that I killed a cow, but also I shot another animal, which carried away three of my arrows. It was afterward killed by a man a long way off, and the next day he gave me back my arrows, which he had taken from the cow. I felt ashamed of this, but, nevertheless, I kept on, and before the hunt was over I killed many buffalo, and my mother dressed the hides.

In the Medicine Circle.

Soon after I had killed my big buffalo, my uncle had sent for me and when I had gone to his lodge, he said, "Come with me"; and we walked out on the prairie where his horses were feeding. He carried a rope in his hand, and, throwing it over the fast buffalo horse, that he had told me to ride when I first hunted buffalo, he put the rope in my hand, and said: "Son, I give you this horse; he is fast, and he is long-winded. You have seen that he can overtake buffalo. I tell you now that he is a good horse for war. If you ride him when you go on the war-path, you can get up close to your enemy, and strike him; he will not be able to run away from you."

This was the first horse I had, and I was proud to own it. Also, later, my uncle said to me, "My son, if you need horses for riding, catch some of those out of my band, and use them." This I did, sometimes. My uncle had plenty of horses, and was always going to war and getting more.

I was now a big boy, and began to think more and more about going to war. Ever since I had been little I had talked with my companions, and they with me, about the time when we should be big enough to do the things that our fathers and uncles did; and the thing that we most wished to do was to go to war against the enemy, and to do something brave, so that we should be looked up to by the people. As we grew older the wish to do this increased. That summer, when the old men used to come out of their lodges, and sit in the sun, smoking, or to gather in little groups, and gossip with one another, I used to listen to their talk of the things that had happened in past years, when they were young. They told of many strange things that had happened; of war journeys that they had made against their enemies, of fights that they had had, and horses that they had taken. They spoke, too, of treaties that they had made with other tribes; and told how they had visited the camps of people who lived far off, whose names I had heard, but of whom I knew nothing.

Sometimes, too, I was present in my uncle's lodge when he gave a feast to friends; and often among them were chiefs and older men, who in their day had done great things, and brought credit to the tribe. At such feasts, after all had eaten, and my uncle had filled the pipe, and pushed the tobacco board back under the bed, he gave the pipe to some young man, who lighted it and handed it back to him; and then he smoked, holding the pipe to the sky, and to the earth, and to the four directions, and made a prayer to the spirits, and then passed the pipe along to the end of the circle on his left; and, beginning there, each man smoked and made a prayer, and the pipe passed from hand to hand. After this the guests talked and joked, and laughed, and stories were told, perhaps of war or adventure, perhaps of hard times when food was scarce and the cold bitter, perhaps of those mysterious persons who rule the world, and of the kindly or the terrible things that they have done.

I remember well one such feast, when for the first time my uncle told me to sit on his right hand, and behind him; and when he had filled it, told me to light the pipe. I reached over to the fire, and with a tongs made of willow took up a small coal and lighted the pipe, and after it was going well, passed it to my uncle. And so I lighted all the pipes that were smoked that night. It was during the second of these pipes that an old man, Calf Robe, told a story of a thing that had happened in the tribe long ago, when he was a young man. He was a little man, thin and dried up, but in his time he had been a great warrior. Now he was old and poor, his left arm thin, withered and helpless, and on his side a great scar, much larger than my two hands, where people said his ribs on that side had all been torn away. I had heard of his adventures, how once the animals had taken pity on him, and brought him, after he was sorely wounded on a war journey, safe back to his people and his village. It was on this night that I first heard the story of the Medicine Circle. This was what he said:

"It was winter. The people were camped on Lodgepole Creek near the Big Horn Mountains. Buffalo were close and small game plenty. The snow was deep, and the people did not watch their horses closely, for they thought no war parties would be out in such cold and in such deep snow.

"The chief of this camp had strong mysterious power.

When Buffalo Ran.

On the ground at the right of his bed in his lodge was always a space, where red painted wooden pegs were set in the ground in a circle. Above this hung the medicine bundles. No one was allowed to step or sit in this circle. No one might throw anything on the ground near it. No one might pass between it and the fire. It was sacred.

"It was a very cold night. The wind blew the snow about so that one could hardly see. The chief had gone to a feast in a lodge near his own, and his wives were in bed, but one of them was still awake. The fire had burned down, and the lodge was almost dark. Suddenly the curtain of the doorway was thrown back. A person entered, passed around to the back of the lodge, and sat down in the medicine circle.

" 'Now what is this?' the woman thought; 'why does this person sit in the medicine circle?'

"She said to him: 'You know that is the medicine circle. Quick! get up, and sit down somewhere else. My husband will be angry if he sees you there.'

"The person did not speak nor move, so the woman got up and put grass on the fire, and when it made a light, she saw that the man was a stranger, for his clothing was different from ours; but she could not see his face; he kept it covered, all but his eyes. The woman went out and ran to the lodge where her husband was, and said to him: 'Come quickly! A stranger has entered our lodge. He is sitting in the medicine circle.'

"The chief went to his lodge, and many with him—for chiefs and warriors had been feasting together—and

HOLDING THE PIPE TO THE SKY AND TO THE EARTH

they carried in more wood and built a big fire. Then the stranger moved toward the fire, nearer and nearer, and they saw he was shaking with cold. His moccasins and leggings were torn and covered with ice, and his robe was thin and worn.

"The chief was greatly troubled to see this person sitting in his medicine circle, and he asked him in signs, 'Where did you come from?'

"He made no answer.

"Again he asked, 'Who are you?'

"The stranger did not speak. He sat as close to the fire as he could get, still shivering with cold.

"The chief told a woman to feed him; and she warmed some soup and meat over the fire, and set it before the stranger. Then he threw off his robe, and began to eat like a dog that is starved; and all the people sat and looked at him. He was a young man; his face was good, and his hair very long; but he looked thin, and his clothes were poor.

"The stranger ate all the soup and meat, and then he spoke, in signs: 'I came from the north. I was with a large party. We traveled south many days, and at last saw a big camp by a river. At night we went down to it, to take horses, but I got none, and my party rode off and left me. They told me to go with them and they would give me some of the horses that they had taken, but I was ashamed. I had taken no horses, and I could not go back to my people without counting a coup. So I came on alone, and it is now many days since I left my party. I had used up all my arrows, and could kill no food. I began to starve. To-day I saw your camp. I thought to take some horses from you, but my arrows are gone; I should have starved on the road. My clothes are thin and torn; I should have frozen. So I made up my mind to come to your camp and be killed.

"'Come, I am ready. Kill me! I am a Blackfoot.'

"A pipe was filled, lighted, and passed around. But the chief sat thinking. Everyone was waiting to hear what he would say.

"At last he spoke: 'An enemy has come into our camp. The Blackfeet are our enemies. They kill us when they can. We kill them. This man came here to steal our horses, and he ought to be killed. But, you see, he has come into my lodge and sat down in the medicine circle. Perhaps his medicine led him to the place. He must have a powerful helper.

"'There are many lodges in this camp, and in each of these lodges many seats, but he has come to my lodge, and has sat down in my medicine circle. I believe my medicine helped him too. So now I am afraid to kill this man, for if I do, it may break my medicine. I have finished.'

"Everyone said the chief's talk was good. The chief turned to the Blackfoot and said: 'Do not be afraid; we will not kill you. You are tired. Take off your leggings and moccasins, and lie down in that bed.'

"The Blackfoot did as he was told, and as soon as he lay down he slept; for he was very tired.

In the Medicine Circle.

"Next morning, when he awoke, there by his bed were new leggings for him, and warm hair moccasins, and a new soft cow's robe; and he put these on, and his heart was glad. Then they ate, and the chief told him about the medicine circle, and why they had not killed him.

"In the spring a party of our people went to war against the Crows and the Blackfoot went with them, and he took many horses. He went to war often, and soon had a big band of horses. He married two women of our tribe, and stayed with us. Sometimes they used to ask him if he would ever go back to his people, and he would say: 'Wait, I want to get more horses, and when I have a big band—a great many—I will take my lodge, and my women and children, and we will go north, and I will make peace between your tribe and the Blackfeet.'

"One summer the people were running buffalo. They were making new lodges. One day the men went out to hunt. At sundown they came back, but the Blackfoot did not return. Next day the men went out to look for him, and they searched all over the country. Many days they hunted for the Blackfoot, but he was never seen again. Some said he had gone back to his people. Some said that a bear might have killed him, or he might have fallen from his horse and been killed, and some said that a war party must have killed him and taken the horse with them. Neither man nor horse was seen again."

Among Enemy Lodges.

It was late in the winter, when I was fifteen years old, that I made my first trip to war. We were camped on a large river, and not far from our camp was a village of the Arapahoes.

One day I went to visit their camp, taking with me only my buffalo robe and my bow and arrows. At the camp I found a number of young men of my tribe, and I went into the lodge where they were sitting, and sat down near the door. Soon after I had entered a young man of my tribe proposed that our young men should gamble against the young men of the Arapahoes, and when they had agreed, we all left the lodge where we were sitting, and went off to that owned by Shaved-head. I followed along after the others, and when I entered the lodge I found that they were making ready to gamble. The counters were lying between the lines, ten of the sticks lying side by side, and two lying across the ten.

When all was ready, the leader of the Arapahoes threw down on the ground the bone they were to gamble with, and the leader of our young men threw down his bone, and then all the young men of both parties began to sing, and dance, and yell, each trying to bring luck to his side. Some of them danced all around the lodge, singing as hard as they could sing. After a time all sat down, and then one of the Arapahoes chose a man from his side, and called him out and told him to sit down in front of his line. The leader took up the bone, and held it up to the sun, and to the four directions, praying that his side might win, and then handed it to this man, who let the robe fall back from his shoulders, rose to his knees, and after rubbing his hands on the ground, began to pass the bone from one hand to the other. Then the leader of our party stood up, and looked over his men, to choose someone who was good at guessing. He chose a man, and called him out in front of the line, to guess in which hand the Arapahoe held the bone. Then everybody began to sing hard, and four young men pounded with sticks on a parfleche, in time to the music. Presently our man guessed and guessed right. Then our people chose a man to pass the bone for them, and when the Arapahoes guessed, they guessed wrong. So it kept on. The Arapahoes did not win one point, and our people won the game. Then the Arapahoes would play no more, and the gambling stopped. Afterward they had a dance.

It was now night. I had heard the young men talking to one another, and I knew that they were about to start off to war. After the dance was over, one of them said to the others, "Come, let us go about the camp to-night, and sing wolf songs." They did so, and I went with them. Every little while they would stop in front of some lodge and sing; and perhaps the man who owned the lodge would fill a pipe, and hold it out to them, and all would smoke; or someone would hand out a bit of tobacco, or a few arrows, or five or six bullets, or some caps, or a little powder. In this way they sang for a long time; and then, when they were tired, they went to the different lodges and slept.

The next morning I saw them making up the packs which they were to carry on their backs, and packing the dogs which they had with them to carry their moccasins. I watched them, and as I looked at them I wished that I, too, might go to war; and the more I thought about it the more I wished to go. At last I made up my mind that I would go. I had no food, and no extra moccasins, but I looked about the camp, and found some that had been thrown away, worn out; and I asked one kind-hearted woman to give me some moccasins, and she gave me three pairs. By this time the war party had started, and I followed them.

The snow still lay deep on the ground; and as we marched along, one after another, each man stepped in the tracks of the man before him. We traveled a long way, until we came to some hills, from which we could see a river; and before we got down to the river's valley we stopped on a hill, and took off our packs, and looked about and rested. After a time someone said, "Well, let us go down to the river and camp." They all started down the hill, but I remained where I was, waiting to see what they would do. You see, I did not belong to the party, and I did not know how the others felt toward me; so I was shy about doing anything; I wanted to wait and see what they did.

When the others reached the level ground near the

stream they threw down their packs and began to go to work. Some of the men scraped away the snow from the ground where they were to sleep; others went off into the timber, and soon returned with loads of wood on their backs, and started fires; others brought poles with which to build lodges; others, bark from old cottonwood trees, and others, still, brush. Everyone worked hard.

Presently I grew tired of sitting alone on the hill, and went down to the others. When I reached there, I found that they were building three war lodges, and as I drew near, all the young men began to call out to me, each one asking me to come over to him. I was the littlest fellow in the party, and they all wanted me, thinking that I might bring them luck. When they called to me, they did not speak to me by my name, but called me Bear Chief, the name of one of the greatest warriors of the tribe. They were joking with me, to tease me.

When I was near the lodges I stopped, uncertain what to do, or where to go, and Gray Eyes, a man a little older than the others, walked up to me, and took me by the arm, saying: "Friend, come to our lodge. If you go to one of the others, the young men will be making fun of you all the time." I went to his lodge, and he told me to sit down near the door. This lodge was well built, warm and comfortable. They had taken many straight poles and set them up as the poles of a lodge are set up, but much closer together. Then the poles were covered with bark and brush, so as to keep out the wind; and within, all about the lodge, were good beds, with bark and brush under them, so as to keep those who were to sleep there from the snow. A good fire burned in the middle of the lodge.

When I grew warm I began to wonder what we should have to eat. We had traveled all day, and I was hungry; yet I had no food, and could see none, and there was nothing to cook with, not even a kettle. A man sitting by the fire seemed to know what was in my mind, and said to me, "Take courage, friend, soon you shall have plenty to eat." A little while after this, a man called out, saying, "If anyone has food to eat, let him get it out." When he said that, the young men began to open their packs. While they were doing this, someone cried, "The hunters are coming"; and when I looked I saw three or four men coming, each with an antelope on his back. When these men had come near to the camp, everyone rushed for them, and they threw their loads on the snow, and each man cut off meat for his lodge. Then they cut it into pieces and it was set up on green willow twigs, stuck in the ground near the fire, to roast. One of the men in our lodge said, "Let our young friend here be the first one to eat," and someone cut a piece of the short ribs of an antelope, and gave it to me. So we all ate, and were warm and comfortable. That night we slept well, lying with our feet to the fire, as people always lie in a war lodge.

The next day we traveled on. Just before we camped at night I heard the sound of guns, and someone told me that the young men were killing buffalo. Soon after we had made camp, they began to come in, some carrying loads of meat on their backs, and others dragging over the snow a big piece of buffalo hide, sewed up into a sack, and full of meat. Everyone was good-natured, and each young man was laughing and joking with his fellows, and sometimes playing tricks on them. That night a friend took a piece of buffalo hide and sewed it up, and partly dried it over the fire, and then turned it inside out, and stuffed it full of meat, and gave it to me, saying, "Here is a pack for you to carry."

We traveled on for several days; but it was not long after this that the scouts came in, and told us that they had seen signs of people, a trail where a large camp had passed along only a few days before. When I heard this I was a little frightened, for I thought to myself, "Suppose we were to be attacked, how could I run away with this big pack on my back?" But I said nothing, and no one else seemed to be afraid; all were happy because there was a chance that we might meet enemies. They laughed and talked with one another, and said what a good time we should have if there should be a fight. Nevertheless, that night the leader told the young men to bring logs out of the timber, and pile them up around the war lodges, so that if we should be attacked we might fight behind breast works. Also, he told them that if we should be attacked we must not run out of the lodges, but must stay in them, where we could fight well, and be protected and safe. Also, he said, "Everyone must be watchful; it may be that enemies are near; therefore, act accordingly."

Among Enemy Lodges.

The next morning the leader sent out two parties of scouts, to go in two directions to look for enemies. He told them where they should go, and where they should meet the main party, which was to keep on its way, traveling carefully, and out of sight.

At night, after we had reached the appointed place, and had camped there, the scouts came in, and told us that they had found the enemy, and that their camp was not far off. When the leader learned that, he said, "It will be well for us to go to-night to the camp of these enemies, and try to take their horses." The distance was not great, and after we had eaten, all set out. When we had come near to the camp, we could see in some of the lodges the fires still burning, and knew that all the people had not gone to bed. In a low place we stopped, and there put down all our things. Here the leader told us what we must do, calling out by name certain men who should go into the camp, and certain other men, younger, who should go about through the hills and gather up loose horses, and drive them to the place where we had left our packs. My name he did not speak, and I did not know what to do. While I sat there, doubtful, all the others started off. Then I made up my mind that I, too, would go into the camp, and would try to do something, and I followed the others. After a little time I overtook them, and followed along, and as we went on and drew nearer and nearer to the camp, men kept turning off to one side, until presently, when we were quite near the camp, most of them had disappeared into the darkness;

but I could still see some, walking along ahead of me. Presently we reached the outer circle of the lodges, and a moment or two after that I could see none of our people. I was walking alone among the lodges. Now I was afraid, for I did not know how to act, nor what I wanted to do, and I thought that perhaps one of the enemy might see me, and see that I did not belong to his tribe, and attack me and kill me. I held my head down, and walked straight along. Not many people were about, and no one passed me. Presently I came to a lodge in which a little fire was burning, and not very far away was another lodge, in which people were singing and drumming, as if for a dance. I stopped, and looked into the first lodge. The fire was low, but still it gave some light, and I could see plainly that no one was there. Then suddenly it came to me that I would go into this lodge, and take something out of it, which should show to my friends that I, too, had been in the camp. I did not think much of the danger that someone might come in, but, stooping down, entered the lodge, and looked about. Hanging over the bed, at the back of the lodge, was a bow-case and quiver full of arrows. I stepped quickly across and took this down, and putting it under my robe, went out of the lodge, and walked back the way I had come.

As I had entered the camp I had seen horses standing, tied in front of the lodges, and now, as I was going back, I stooped down in front of a lodge, where all was dark, cut loose a horse, and walked away, leading it by its rope. No one saw me, and when I had passed beyond the furthest lodge I mounted the horse and rode along slowly. After I had gone a little further, I went faster, and soon I was at the place where we had left our things. There were many horses there, brought in by the younger men that had been looking for loose horses, and some cut loose by those who had gone into camp. Every minute other men kept coming up, and presently all were there. The young men had filled their saddle-pads with grass, and now each one chose a good horse, and mounting it drove off the herd. I had only one horse, yet my heart was glad, for it was the first I had ever taken.

For a time we rode slowly, but presently, faster; and when day had come we had gone a long way. The horses were still being driven in separate bunches, so that each man should know which were his—the ones he had taken; but soon after day broke, and there had been time for each to look over his animals, they were bunched to-gether, and we went faster. Nevertheless, the leader said to us: "Friends, do not hurry the horses too much; they are poor, and we must not run them too hard. The horses on which the Crows will follow us are poor also, and they cannot overtake us."

We rode fast until afternoon, when we came down into the valley of a river, and there stopped to let our horses feed. Two young men with fresh horses were left behind, on top of the highest hills, to watch the trail, to see whether the enemy were following us. After we had been there for a time, and the horses had eaten, the leader called out, "Friends, the enemy are pursuing; we must hurry on the horses." In a moment we had caught our animals, and mounted, and were driving on the herd; for, far back, we could see the scouts who had been left behind coming toward us, riding fast, and making signs that people had been seen. After we had left the valley, and were among the hills, the leader left two other young men, on fresh horses, behind, to see whether the enemy crossed the river, and followed; while we went on with the horses. We rode all that night and part of the next day, and then stopped again; and that night, in the middle of the night, the scouts overtook us, and told us that the enemy had not crossed the river, where we had first slept, but had turned about there, and had gone back. "There were only a few of them," they said. "We two were almost tempted to attack them, but we had been told only to watch them, and we thought it better to do that." Four days afterward we reached our village.

I had no saddle, and when I reached the camp I was very sore and stiff from riding so long without a saddle. Nevertheless, I was pleased, for I had taken a horse that was fast, long-winded and tough; and I had taken also a fine bow and arrows, with an otter-skin case. The leader spoke to me, and told me that I had done well to go into this lodge. He said to me, "Friend, you have made a good beginning; I think that you will be a good warrior." Also, when we reached the village, my uncle praised me, and said that I had done well. He looked at the bow and the arrows, and told me that to have taken them was better than to have taken a good horse, and that he hoped that I would be able to use them in fighting with my enemies. Such was my first journey to war.

A Grown Man.

THAT summer my uncle gave me a gun, and now I was beginning to feel that I was really a man, and I hunted constantly, and had good luck, killing deer and elk, and other game.

One day the next year, with a friend, I was hunting a two days' journey from the camp. We had killed nothing until this day, when we got a deer, and toward evening stopped to cook and eat. The country was broken with many hills and ravines, and before we went down to the stream to build our fire I had looked from the top of a little hill, to see whether anything could be seen. My friend was building a fire to cook food, and I had gone down to the fire and spread my robe on the ground, and was lying on it, resting, while our horses were feeding near by, when suddenly I had a strange feeling. I seemed to feel that I was in great danger, and as if I must get away from this place. I was frightened. I felt there was danger; that something bad was going to happen. I did not know what it was, nor why I felt so, but I was afraid. I seemed to turn to water inside of me. I had never felt so before. I sat up and looked about; nothing was to be seen. My friend was cutting some meat to cook over the little fire, and just beyond him the horses were feeding. My friend was singing to himself a little war song, as he worked.

My feelings grew worse instead of better. I stood up, took my gun, and walked toward a little hill not far from where we were, and my friend called out to me, "Where are you going? I thought you wished to rest." I said to him, "I will go to the top of that little hill, and look over it." When I got there I looked about; I could see nothing. It was early summer, and the grass was green. The soil was soft and sandy. For a long time I looked about in all directions, but could see nothing, but then I could not see far, for there were other little hills, nearly as high, close to me.

Presently I looked at the ground a few steps before me, and I thought I saw where something had stepped. It was hard for me to make up my mind to walk to this place, but at length I did so. When I got there I saw where a horse had stood—a fresh horse track. Near it were two tracks made by a man, an enemy. I could see where he had stood, with one foot advanced before the other. When I saw these tracks I knew what had happened; an enemy had stood there looking over at us, and when he saw me with my gun start toward the top of the hill he had gone away. Standing where he had stood, I looked back toward our horses; I could hardly see their backs, but a man taller than I could have seen more of them, and the heads of the two men. I turned to follow the tracks a little way, and as I walked, it did not seem to me that my bones were stiff enough to support my body; I seemed to sway from side to side, and felt as if I should fall down. I was frightened.

A Grown Man.

I saw where the man had led his horse a little way back from the hill, and then had jumped on it and ridden off as hard as he could gallop. A little further on was the place where another horse had stood; it, too, had turned and gone off fast; its rider had not dismounted. One of the men had said to the other: "You wait here, and I will go up and take a look. If these people sleep here we will attack them when it is dark, and kill them and take their horses."

I cannot tell you how much I wanted to run back to my friend and tell him what I had seen; but I had courage enough to walk. I felt angry at myself for being so frightened. I said to myself: "Come, you are a man; you belong to brave people; your uncle and your father did not fear things that they could not see. Be brave. Be strong." It was no use for me to say this; I was so frightened I could hardly control myself. I felt as if I must run away.

I walked until I was close to my friend. He was cooking meat, and was still singing to himself. When I was pretty near to him I said, "Friend, put the saddle on your horse, and I will saddle mine, and we will go away from here." He turned and looked at me, and in a moment he had dropped the meat that he was cooking, and was saddling up. He told me the next day that my face had changed so that he hardly knew me; my face was like that of one dead. I said to him, "Do you go ahead, and go fast, but do not gallop." He started off without a word, and I followed him. It was now growing dark, but you could still see a long way. As I rode I seemed to have three heads, I looked in so many different directions. We traveled fast. My courage did not come back to me. I was still miserable.

About the middle of the night I said to my friend, "Let us stop here, so that the horses may eat." We stopped and took off our saddles, and held the ropes of our horses in our hands, and lay down on the ground together, looking back over the trail that we had come. My friend's horse was eating, but mine stood with his head high, and his ears pricked, and kept looking back toward where we had come from. Every now and then he would snort, as if frightened. Sometimes he would take a bite or two of grass, and then would again stand with his head up, looking and snorting. This made me more afraid than ever; and now my friend was as badly frightened as I.

At last I could stand it no longer, and I said to him, "Let us turn off the trail, and go along a divide where no one is likely to follow us." We started, loping. After we had gone some distance we stopped, took off our bridles, and again lay down, looking back over the way we had come. The night was dark, but we could see a little, and we watched and listened. Still my horse would not eat, but kept looking back over the trail. Suddenly, my friend said, "There he is. Do you see?" I looked, and looked, but could see nothing. "Where is it?" said I. With my head close to the ground I looked in the direction in which he pointed, but could see nothing. My friend saw it

76

move, however. I said to him, "Here, let us change places;" and I moved to his place, and he to mine. Then I looked, and in a moment I saw just in front of my face a weed-stalk, and when I moved my head the stalk moved. This was what he had seen.

For the first time since this feeling had come over me in the afternoon I laughed, and with a rush my courage came back to me. I felt as brave and cheerful as ever. All through the evening I had not wished to smoke, and if I had wished to, I should have been afraid to light my pipe. Now I filled my pipe, lighted it, and we smoked. When I laughed my friend's courage came back too. We lay down and slept, and the next day went on to the village.

A Sacrifice.

During the next two years I went to war five times, always as a servant, but always I had good luck. This was because early, after my first trip to war, I had asked an old man, one of my relations, to teach me how to make a sacrifice which should be pleasing to those spirits who rule the world.

It was in the early summer, when the grass was high and green, not yet turning brown, that, with this old man, Torn Lodge, I went out into the hills to suffer and to pray, to ask for help in my life, and that I might be blessed in all my warpaths. Torn Lodge had told me what I must do, and before the time came I had cut a pole, and brought it and a rope, and a bundle of sinew, and some small wooden pins near to the place where we were to go, and had hidden them in a ravine.

It was before the sun had risen that we started out, and when we came to the hill where the things were, I carried them to the top of the hill, and there Torn Lodge and I dug a hole in the soil with our knives, and planted the pole, stamping the earth tightly about it, and then putting great stones on the earth, so that the pole should be held firmly. Then Torn Lodge tied the rope to the pole, and with sinew tied the pins to the rope, and then holding the pins and his knife up to the sun, and to the sky, and then placing them on the earth, he prayed to all the spirits of the air, and of the earth, and of the waters, asking that this sacrifice that I was about to make should be blessed, and that I should have help in all my undertakings. Then he came and stood before me, and taking hold of the skin of my breast on the right side, he pinched it up and passed his knife through it, and then passed the pin through under the skin, and tied the end to the rope with another strand of sinew. In the same way he did on the left side of my breast. Then he told me that all through the day I should walk about this pole, always on the side of the pole toward which the sun was looking, and that I should throw myself back against the rope and should try to tear the pins from my skin. Then, telling me to pray constantly, to have a strong heart, and not to lose courage, he set out to return to the village.

All through the long summer day I walked about the pole, praying to all the spirits, and crying aloud to the sun and the earth, and all the animals and birds to help me. Each time when I came to the end of the rope I threw myself back against it, and pulled hard. The skin of my breast stretched out as wide as your hand, but it would not tear, and at last all my chest grew numb, so that it had no feeling in it; and yet, little by little, as I threw my whole weight against the rope, the strips of skin stretched out longer and longer. All day long I walked in this way. The sun blazed down like fire. I had no food, and did not drink; for so I had been instructed. Toward night my mouth grew dry, and my neck sore;

"DO NOT GO; WAIT A LITTLE LONGER"

so that to swallow, or even to open my mouth in prayer hurt me. It seemed a long time before the sun got overhead and the pole cast but a small shadow; but it seemed that the shadow of the pole grew long in the afternoon much more slowly than it had grown short in the morning.

I was very tired, and my legs were shaking under me, when at last, as the sun hung low over the western hills, I saw someone coming. It was my friend, Torn Lodge; and when he had come close to me, he spoke to me and said, "My son, have you been faithful all through the day?" I answered him, "Father, I have walked and prayed all day long, but I cannot tear out these pins." "You have done well," he said; and, drawing his knife, he came to me, and taking hold first of one pin and then of the other, he cut off the strips of skin which passed about the pins, and set me free. He held the strips of skin that he had cut off, toward the sky, and toward the four directions, and prayed, saying: "Listen! all you spirits of the air, and of the earth, and of the water; and you, O earth! and you, O sun! This is the sacrifice that my son has made to you. You have heard how he cries to you for help. Hear his prayer." Then at the foot of the pole he scraped a little hole in the earth and placed the bits of skin there, and covered them up. Then he gave me to drink from a buffalo paunch waterskin that he had brought.

"Now, my son," said he, "you shall sleep here this night, and to-morrow morning, as the sun rises, leave this hill, and everything on it, as it is, and return to the camp. It may be that during the night something will come to you, to tell you a thing. If you are spoken to in your sleep, remember carefully what is said to you."

After he had gone I lay down, covering myself with my robe, and was soon asleep, for I was very tired. That night, while I slept, I dreamed that a wolf came to me, and spoke, saying: "My son, the spirits to whom you have cried all day long have heard your prayers, and have sent me to tell you that your cryings have not been in vain. Take courage, therefore, for you shall be fortunate so long as these wars last. You shall strike your enemies; your name shall be called through the camp, and all your relations will be glad.

"Look at me, and consider well my ways. Remember that of all the animals, the wolves are the smartest. If they get hungry, they go out and kill a buffalo; they know what is going to happen; they are always able to take care of themselves. You shall be like the wolf; you shall be able to creep close to your enemies, and they shall not see you; you shall be a great man for surprising people. In the bundle that you wear tied to your necklet, you shall carry a little wolf hair, and your quiver and your bow-case shall be made of the skin of a wolf." The wolf ceased speaking, yet for a time he sat there looking at me, and I at him; but presently he yawned, and stood up on his feet, and trotted off a little way, and suddenly I could not see him.

So then in these five times that I went to war, once I

counted the first coup of all on an enemy; and three times I crept into camp and brought out horses, twice going with other men who went in to cut loose the horses, and once going in alone. For these things I came to be well thought of by the tribe. My uncle praised me, and said that the time was coming when I would be a good warrior. All my relations felt proud and glad that I had such good luck.

I knew why all this had come to me. I had done as the wolf had said, and often I went out from the camp—or perhaps I stopped when I was traveling far from the village—and went up on a hill, and, lighting a pipe, offered a smoke to the wolf, and asked him not to forget what he had said to me.

I was now a grown man, and able to do all the things that young men do. I was a good hunter; I had a herd of horses, and had been to war, and been well spoken of by the leaders whose war parties I went with. I was old enough, too, to think about young girls, and to feel that some day I wanted to get married, and to have a lodge and home of my own. There were many nice girls in the camp; many who were hard workers, modest, and very pretty. I liked many of them, but there was no one whom I liked so much as Standing Alone. I often saw her, but sometimes she would not look at me, and sometimes she looked, but when she saw me looking at her she looked down again; but sometimes she smiled a little as she looked down. It was long since we had played together, but I thought that perhaps she had not forgotten the time, so many years ago, when she pretended to be my wife, and when she had mourned over me once when I was killed by a buffalo.

As I grew older I felt more and more that I wished to see and talk with her. Of course I was too young to be married yet, but I was not too young to want to talk with Standing Alone. I used to go out and stand by the trail where the women passed to get water, hoping that I might speak to her, but often there was no chance to do so. Sometimes she was with other girls, who laughed and joked about me, and asked whom I was waiting for. They could not tell who was standing there, for my robe or my sheet covered my whole body, except the hole through which I looked with one eye. But one day when Standing Alone was going by with some girls, one of them recognized the sheet that I had on, and called out my name, and said that she believed that I was waiting for Standing Alone. I was surprised that she should know me, and felt badly, but I did not move, and so I think neither she nor the girls with her knew that she had guessed right; and the next time I went I wore a different sheet, and different moccasins and leggings.

One evening I had good luck; all the women had passed, and Standing Alone had not appeared. I supposed that all had got their water, and was about to go away when she came hurrying along the trail, and passed me and went to the water's edge. She filled her vessel and came back, and when she passed me again I took hold of her dress and pulled it, and dropped my sheet from my head. She stopped and we stood there and talked for a little while. We were both of us afraid, we did not know of what, and had not much to say, but it was pleasant to be there talking to her, and looking at her face. Three times she started to go, but each time I said to her, "Do not go; wait a little longer"; and each time she waited. The fourth time she went away. After that, I think she knew me whenever I stood by the trail, and sometimes she was late in coming for water, and I had a chance to speak to her alone.

In those days I was happy; and often when the camp was resting, and there was nothing for me to do, I used to go out and sit on the top of a high hill, and think about Standing Alone, and hope that in the time to come I might have her for my wife, and that I might do great things in war, so that she would be proud of me; and might bring back many horses for her, so that she could always ride a good horse, and have a finely orna-mented saddle and saddle-cloth. If I could take horses enough, I should be rich, and then whatever Standing Alone might desire, I could give a horse for it.

A Warrior Ready to Die.

It was not long after this that buffalo were found, and we began to kill them, as we used to do in the old times; and then a great misfortune happened to me.

One day I was chasing buffalo on a young horse, and as it ran down a steep hill, it stumbled among the stones, and fell down, rolling over, and I was thrown far; and, as I fell to the ground, my knee struck against a large stone. When I got up my leg was useless, and I could not walk, but I managed to catch my horse, and crawling on it I reached the camp. After a little my knee got better, and then again worse, and then better again. Still I could not walk, and for two years I stayed in the camp, crippled, and unable to go from place to place, except when I was helped on my horse. I grew thin and weak, and thought that I should die.

Many of the young men of my age, my friends, were sorry for me. They used to come to my lodge and eat and talk, telling me the news. Sometimes, when I was sitting out in the shade of the lodge, looking over the camp, and feeling the pleasant breeze blow on my face, or the warm sun shine on my body, I saw the young men and boys walking about, and running, and wrestling, and kicking, and jumping on their horses and galloping off, and it made me feel badly to think that I could no longer do the things that I used to do; could no longer hunt, and help to support my relations; could no longer go off on the warpath with my fellows, to fight the enemy, or to take plunder from them. I was useless.

Often during this time, older men—my uncle's friends —used to come to the lodge, and stop there and talk with me for a little time, to cheer me up, for I think they too felt sorry for me. The doctors tried hard to cure my leg, but though they did many things, and I and my uncle paid them many horses, and saddles and blankets, they could not help me. Once in a while, in the morning, after all the men had gone out to chase buffalo, or to hunt for smaller animals, deer or elk or antelope, Standing Alone would come to my mother's lodge, perhaps bringing some little present for her, and would sit and talk with her, and sometimes look at me, and I could see that her eyes were full of tears, and that she too felt sorry. Sometimes she spoke to me, but not often; but it always made me glad to see her, and made me feel more than ever that she had a good heart.

At the end of two years I sent word to my uncle, asking him to come to see me; and when he had come and sat down, I asked my mother and my sisters to leave the lodge, and when they had gone I spoke to my uncle. "Father, you have seen how it has been with me for two years; that I am no longer able to go about; that I am a cripple, lying here day after day, useless to my relations, and very unhappy. Now, I have thought of this for a long time, and I have made up my mind what I shall do. It is time for me to go off with some of the young men on the warpath, and when we meet the enemy, I will ride straight into the midst of them, and will strike one, and he shall kill me. I am no longer glad to live, and it will be well for me to die bravely."

For a long time my uncle said nothing, but sat there looking at the ground. After he had thought, he raised his head and spoke to me, saying: "Son, you can remember how it has been with us since you were a little boy. You have been my son, and I have loved you. I have been glad when you went to war, and glad when you returned with credit; yet I should not have mourned if you had been killed in battle, for that is the way a man ought to die. I have seen your sufferings now for two years, and I know how you feel. I think that it will be well for you to do as you have said, and for you to give your body to the enemy, and to be killed on the open prairie, where the birds and the beasts may feed on your flesh, and may scatter it over the plain. Now, when you are ready to do this, tell me, so that I may see that you go to war as becomes a warrior who is about to die."

It was not very long after this that a party of young men set out to war, all mounted, to go south to look for the Utes. Among them was the one who had been my close friend, and to him I had told what was in my mind; and when I spoke to the leader of the party, he was glad to have me go with him, as were all of them.

I told my uncle, and he gave me his best war horse to ride, and gave me also a sacred headdress that he wore, which had in it some of the feathers of the thunder bird. I took with me no arms, except a stone axe that my father had had from his father, and he from his father, and which had come down in our family through many generations.

The party started, and we traveled fast and far to the south. At first I was very weak, and got very tired during the long marches, but after a time I grew stronger, and could eat better, and felt better; but my leg was as bad as ever.

We had been out many days and were still traveling south, east of the mountains, when, one day our scouts came upon the carcasses of buffalo that had been killed only a little time before, and the meat cut from the bones. From this we knew that enemies were close by, and we went carefully. Not far beyond these carcasses, as we rode up on a hill, we saw before us in the valley two persons butchering a buffalo, and as we watched them at their work, we could see that they were Utes—enemies. All the young men jumped on their horses, and we charged down on them. Before we were near them they had seen us, and had run to their horses, and jumped on them and ridden away. By this time I was far ahead of my friends, for my horse was the fastest of all; and soon I was getting close to these enemies. They rode almost side by side, but one a little ahead of the other.

The one who was on the left and a little behind carried a bow and arrows, while the man on the right had a gun. I said to myself: "I will ride between these two persons, and the man with the bow will then have to shoot toward his right hand, and will very likely miss me, while I may be able to knock him off his horse with my axe." I was not afraid, for I had made up my mind to die.

Before long I had overtaken the Utes, and, riding between them, made ready to strike them. The man with the arrows turned on his horse, and shot at me, but I bent to one side, and the arrow passed by without hitting me, and I struck him with my axe and knocked him off his horse. Then the man with the gun turned and was aiming at me, but when he pulled the trigger his gun snapped and did not go off. I was close to him and caught the barrel in my hand, and struck him with my axe, and knocked him off his horse. Then I rode on, holding his gun in my hand. Before the two men whom I had struck could get on their horses again, my friends had overtaken and killed them.

We traveled on further, but found no more enemies, and at last we gave up, and returned to our village. All the time, as we were journeying about, and going back, I kept feeling better and better. I grew stronger slowly. The swelling on my knee began to go down, so that before we reached the village I could rest my weight on that foot a little. At last we arrived, and when we came in sight of the camp, we could see people looking from the lodges to see who were coming.

As we rode down the hill to charge upon the village, the leader told me to ride far in front, "For," he said, "you are the bravest of all." When we came into the village the men and the women and the children came out to meet us. All of them shouted out my name, and my heart grew big in my breast, for I felt that all the people thought that I had done well. Among the women who came out to meet us, I saw Standing Alone, running along by my mother, and both were singing a glad song. And when I saw this, I came near to crying.

At last I reached my lodge, and before it stood my uncle; and as I rode toward him he called out in a loud voice, and asked a certain man named Brave Wolf to come to his lodge and see his son who had given his body to the enemy, desiring to be killed, but who had done great things and had survived. And when Brave Wolf came to the lodge, my uncle gave to him the best horse that he had, a spotted war pony, handsome and long-winded and fleet.

All that day I sat in the lodge and rested, and talked to my uncle. I told him about our journey to war, and while he did not say much I could see that his heart was glad. Before he got up to leave the lodge, he said to me, "Friend, you have done well; I am glad to have such a son." This made me feel glad and proud—more proud, I think, than I felt when I heard the people shout out my name. I loved my uncle and it seemed good that I had done something that pleased him.

All day long people were coming to our lodge and talking about what had happened to us while on our journey. Those who came were my relations and friends, but, besides these, older men, good warriors, people to whose words all the tribe listened, came and sat and talked with me for a little while. My mother and one or two of her relations were busy all day cooking food for the visitors. It was a happy time.

The leader of our war party sent word to me that this night there would be a war dance over the scalps that had been taken. Although I could walk a little, I could not dance, yet I wished to go to the dance and watch the others. All through the afternoon boys and young men were bringing wood to a level place in the circle of the camp, and there they built what we call a "skunk," piling up long poles together in a shape somewhat like a lodge, so that when finished the "skunk" looked like a war lodge.

Late in the night the people gathered near the "skunk," called together by the sound of the singing and the drumming. Leaning on a stick, I walked down there, and before long the "skunk" was lighted, and the members of our war party and the young women began to dance. Although I could not dance, my face was painted black like those of other men of the war party, and I sat there and watched the young people dance and saw the old men and women carry about the scalps. That was one of the last of the old-fashioned war dances that I ever saw held.

The days went by, and before the birds had flown over on their way to the south, and the weather became cold, I could walk pretty well, and could ride easily. One day about this time a doctor whom I had given many presents a year or two before to cure my sickness came to my lodge and asked me if I did not think I ought to give him a present because he had cured me of the swollen knee that I had had so long. I said to him that I believed that not he but the Great Power, to whom I had prayed and to whom I had offered my body as a sacrifice, had cured me. The doctor said that this was a mistake; that really he had cured me, but that his power had not had time to work until after I had started on my warpath.

I did not think that this was true, but I remembered that this man possessed mysterious power, and I felt that perhaps it would not be wise to refuse what he asked. I told him I must have time to think about this, and that in seven days he should return and I would talk further with him about it. Not long after this I told my uncle what the doctor had said. At first he was angry and said that I would do well to refuse what had been asked of me, but after we had talked about it, he came to think as I thought, that perhaps it would be better to make the doctor a present, rather than to have his ill will, for it was possible that he might be able to harm us. My uncle, therefore, told me to give the doctor a certain horse, and a day or two after that he sent me the horse, to be put with my band and later to be given to the doctor. When he received the horse, the doctor was glad, and he told me that after this he would protect me in case any danger threatened me.

The winter passed, the snow melted, the birds went north in spring, and the buffalo began to get poor. It seemed to me now that I was as strong and well as ever

A Warrior Ready to Die.

I had been. I walked alike on both legs, and was as active as any of the young men. During this summer I joined one of the soldier societies of the tribe, and in this I followed the advice of my uncle, who had belonged to this same society.

A Lie That Came True.

Soon after this something strange happened.

I had a friend named Sun's Road. He was a little younger than I, perhaps eighteen or twenty years old, big enough to have a sweetheart, and there was a girl in the camp that he wished to please. He had been more than once to war and had done well, but he wanted to do still better. He was eager to do great things, to make the people talk about him and say that he was brave and always lucky. Like most other young men, he wished to become a great man.

Our camp was on the South Platte River, a big village of near two hundred lodges. All these had been made during the summer, and were new, white and clean. The camp looked nice, but now the buffalo had all gone away. None were to be found and the people were hungry. They had eaten all the food they had saved and now they were eating their dogs, and most of these were already gone.

One day two boys, each the son of a chief, were out on the prairie hunting, and each killed an antelope and took it to his father's lodge. After these had been cooked the chiefs were called together to feast. There was not enough food to allow them to call any others except the chiefs.

I heard of all this at the time, but it was a good deal

later that Sun's Road told me what he had done and what happened to him about this time. He did not wish me to tell anyone about it, but it is a long time ago and those who were important people at that time are now dead, so I think no harm can be done by telling of it.

After these chiefs had eaten, they talked of the suffering of the people and tried to think what could be done to help them. After a time one of the chiefs came out of the lodge and walked through the camp crying aloud to the people, saying, "Listen, listen, you people; we will all stay in this camp." This he called out again and again as he walked around the circle, so that all might hear him.

After a time Sun's Road heard his name called, and the old man shouted: "Sun's Road, Sun's Road; the chief wishes you to go to his lodge. He wishes you to go out to look for buffalo."

Sun's Road went to the chief's lodge and when he had entered they told him where he should sit, by the door, and gave him a little piece of antelope meat to eat. After he had finished eating, the chief said to him: "We want you to-night to go across the river to the other side, and you shall go to where the pile of bones is, where we had the fight with the Pawnees. On the other side of that hill for a long distance the country is level. Look over that country and see if you can see any buffalo and come back and let us know what you have seen. If you see no buffalo do not go farther; come back from there."

The pile of bones was a breastwork of buffalo bones

built on the top of a very high hill by some Pawnees who many years before had been surrounded there by men of our tribe.

Sun's Road started on his journey. When he came to the river he took off his leggings and moccasins and waded across. It was cold, for by this time it was late in the night. On the other side of the river he put on his leggings and moccasins again and walked on north, sometimes walking, and sometimes trotting for a little way. After he had walked a long distance and it was beginning to get toward morning he felt tired and thought that he would rest for a little while. He looked about for a place to lie down, and found a little bunch of brush behind a small bank, and there unbelted his robe and lay down to sleep for a little while. He had not slept long when his feet became cold and this woke him, and when he raised his head he saw that day was beginning to break. He said to himself: "I must not stay here longer. I am out looking for buffalo for people who are starving. I must not lie here," so he rose and tied up his waist and started on.

He walked on and on and at length he saw the high hill and on it the pile of bones. As he went on he came nearer and nearer, and he walked up the hill until he was close by the pile of bones. Then he stopped, for he was afraid. He was afraid that when he looked over the hill he would see nothing. He wanted to make a great man of himself, and to take back the news that he had seen buffalo, so that the people would call his name and all would say that Sun's Road was smart and was lucky. He was so afraid that he would see nothing when he looked over the hill that he stopped and stood there and thought. He said to himself: "If I shall not see anything and go back, they will all hear of it and my girl will hear of it. They will not think much of me. If I could only see plenty of buffalo, what a great man I should be!"

He went on and when he came to the top of the hill and peeped over, there down below him he saw and counted thirty bulls and a calf. He looked at them and said, "Those are bulls; they are not much, but something." He looked another way, and presently he saw one bull, and then two, and then others far off, scattered—in all five or six. He said again, "These are not many, but they will be some help to the people." A little to his right and down the hill a point of the bluff ran out a little way and this point hid a part of the country beyond, and Sun's Road walked down there just a few steps to see what was over that way. When he got there he looked out into a very pretty, level basin with a stream running through it, and said to himself: "This is a pretty place, a good place for buffalo. There ought to be a great many of them here."

At first he could see none, but he kept on looking and at last far off, just specks, he saw a few—a very few, perhaps ten or fifteen—cows.

For a long time he stood there trying to think what he should tell the chiefs when he went back to the camp. He said to himself: "If I go back and tell them just what I have seen it will be nothing to tell. Now, I want people to think that I am a great man, and I am going to tell them a lie. Yes, I shall have to tell them a lie. I shall tell them that when I looked over the hill I saw those thirty bulls with one calf, but beyond I saw many buffalo—hundreds. I know it is a lie, but I shall have to tell it." Then he turned about and went back.

He traveled fast, walking and trotting, and sometimes running, for he wished to reach the camp before night. It was late in the afternoon when he came to the river, waded across and reached the camp. He went into his father's lodge and sat down. His father was at work making a whetstone. He looked up at his son, and said, "Ha, you have returned," and he turned to his wife and said, "Give our son something to eat." His mother was cooking a little dog, the last one they had, and she gave Sun's Road a piece of it and he ate. Then he took off his moccasins, went over to his bed and lay down, covered himself, and went to sleep. He did not speak, and he made no report to the chiefs. Some children were playing in the lodge, and making a little noise, and his father spoke to them, saying, "Go out, you will wake my son; he is tired and has gone to sleep." Sun's Road slept only for a short time, for the lie that he was going to tell troubled him. Pretty soon he heard one of the old chiefs coming—old Double Head. He could hear him coming, coughing and groaning and clearing his throat, and he knew who it was by the sound. The chief entered the lodge and sat down, and said to Sun's Road's father,

"Has your son returned?" The father replied, "Yes, he is asleep." He filled the pipe and Double Head smoked. Sun's Road lay still. In a few moments he heard another old man coming towards the lodge grunting. He knew who it was—White Cow. He came in, sat down, asked the same question that Double Head had asked, and smoked.

White Cow called to Sun's Road, "Nephew, get up now and tell us what you saw; we are starving."

Sun's Road rolled over, pulled the robe from his head, raised himself on his elbow and said: "I went to the hill of the pile of bones, and on the other side of the hill right over beyond the bones I saw thirty bulls and a calf. Just beyond them, as I looked over, I saw many buffalo."

The old men stood up and went out. Soon he heard them crying out through the camp so that all the people should hear: "Sun's Road has come in. On the other side of the pile of bones he saw thirty bulls and a calf, and just below this he saw many buffalo. Gather in your horses. Get them up. Women, sharpen your knives. Men, whet your arrow points. Tie up your horses, and early in the morning we will go after buffalo. The camp will stay here. All will go on horseback."

Sun's Road was frightened when he heard this, but it was now too late to be sorry for what he had done. Next morning just at break of day, before it was light, all the people were out. The old crier was still shouting out, "Saddle your horses; make ready to start, men, women and all."

Soon all were saddled, and they crossed the river and

went on. The chiefs rode first and everyone was behind them. No one rode ahead of them. They went pretty fast, for all were eager to get to the buffalo.

Pretty soon they came in sight of the pile of bones. Sun's Road could hear the old chiefs talking and saying to each other, "There are the bones; soon we will be there at the buffalo." All the time he kept thinking of the lie that he had told, and remembering that there were only a few buffalo, while he had said that there were many. He did not know what he should do.

When they reached the foot of the hill close to the bones, the chiefs stopped and everyone behind them stopped. All the chiefs got off their horses and sat down in a row and filled the pipe and began to smoke. Soon Sun's Road heard one of them call out: "Sun's Road, Sun's Road, go up to the pile of bones and see if you can see your buffalo now. Let us know if they are there." Then Sun's Road was still more frightened. When he first heard his name called, his heart seemed to stop and then it began to beat so fast that it almost choked him. He did not know what to do. He did not move.

Soon old Standing Water, another chief, called out sharply, "Sun's Road, go to the pile of bones and see if you can see those buffalo; come back and tell us what you see."

Then Sun's Road started and rode up towards the pile of bones. Just as he did so a raven flew over him and began to call "Ca, Ca, Ca." He kept riding on, his heart beating fast, but as he rode he held up his hands to the

103

raven and prayed, "Ah, raven, take pity on me and fetch the buffalo." He held his hands up higher and prayed to the Great Power, "O He amma wihio, you are the one who made the buffalo; take pity on me; you know what I need." Then he rode up to the top of the hill.

The moment his head got to where he could see over the hill, he looked and there he saw thirty bulls and the calf. They had hardly moved at all. Then he went on a step or two further, so that he could see beyond them, and the place that he had seen the day before was just full of buffalo. Again he held up his hands to the sky and said: "O raven, O He amma wihio, you have made my words true. The lie that I told you have made come true."

He turned and rode down the hill towards the chiefs. Before he had reached them, one of them called to him to come right to the middle of the line where they were sitting, and when he had come near, they told him to get off his horse and lead it off to one side and then to come back to the middle of the line. They sent a young man to bring a buffalo chip and he brought one and put it down on the ground before the old chief Standing Water, and then went away. The chief placed it on the ground in front of him, about the length of his arm distant from his knees. Then he filled a pipe. Sun's Road still stood out in front of the line, in sight of all the people. He was still badly frightened, for he did not know what they were

WATCH THE MEN AND OLDER BOYS PLAYING AT STICKS

going to do. He was young, and did not know the ceremonies.

When the pipe was filled, the old chief lighted it and pointed the stem to the east, to the south, to the west and to the north, then up to the sky, and then down to the ground. Then he rested the bowl of the pipe on the buffalo chip and said, "Sun's Road, come here." When he had come close, the chief said, "Take hold of this pipe and draw on it five times." The old man held the pipe, and so did Sun's Road, until he had drawn five times on the pipe. Then the chief said, "Now do you hold the pipe,"and Sun's Road held it while the old man took his hands away, and he said: "Sun's Road, pass your hands all down the stem and over the pipe, and then rub your hands over your face and head, and over your arms and body and legs. Then hand me the pipe." Sun's Road did as he was bade. Then the old man put his hand on the buffalo chip and said to Sun's Road, "Did you see bulls?"

And Sun's Road answered, "I saw them."

The old man pulled in the chip a little way toward himself.

"Did you see cows?"

"I saw them."

The chief moved the chip a little further toward himself.

"Did you see two-year-olds?"

"I saw them."

Standing Water moved the chip a little further toward himself.

"Did you see yearlings?"

"I saw them."

"Did you see small calves?"

"I saw them."

After each answer the chip was moved nearer the chief, and when all the questions had been answered it was close to his body. Then Standing Water lifted up his hands toward the sky and thanked He amma wihio for all his goodness to the people.

Standing Water cleaned out the pipe, emptied the ashes on the chip in four piles and left them there. He put his pipe in its sheath and said to the people: "Now, let none of you people go around toward the left and pass in front of this chip—between it and the camp. Back off and all go around behind it, on the side toward the buffalo. If you should pass in front of it that might make the buffalo all go away." All the people went around it, as they had been told to do.

The chiefs mounted and all rode up on the ridge and all saw the buffalo. The chiefs said: "Now here we will divide into two parties; let half go to the right and half to the left. The chiefs will go straight down from here. Let one party go around below the buffalo, and the other party on the upper side. When you get to your places let all make the charge at the same time."

Sun's Road watched where his girl was riding, and when he saw that she went to the right he went that way too, and she saw him on his fine horse. They charged down on the buffalo and he rode close to a fat cow and killed it.

The people killed plenty of buffalo and took much meat back to the camp and ate, and all were happy.

A day or two afterward someone who was out saw the buffalo quite close and coming toward the river. They went out and chased them and again killed plenty. Two or three days later the buffalo began to come down to the river and then to cross the river and to feed in the hills about the camp. The people stayed in this camp for a long time and killed many buffalo and made plenty of robes.

My Marriage.

THE next summer I went with a party to war against the Mexicans. There were seventeen men, and two of them, Howling Wolf and Red Dog, had taken their wives with them. We took many horses, and were coming back, when, while we were passing through the mountains, two of the young men who had been sent ahead as scouts came hurrying back and told us that they had been seen by a camp of enemies, and that many of them were coming. We had a little time, and perhaps if the leaders of the party had been willing to give up the horses we were driving and had told each man to catch his fastest horse, we might have run away, but the leaders did not like to leave the horses and determined to fight those who were coming. Before long we saw them, Utes and Mountain Apaches, a large party—too many for us to fight with. We started to run.

Our horses were tired, and it was not long before our enemies began to overtake us and some of them to strike us with their whips, counting coups. Howling Wolf, a brave man, rode behind us all, trying to defend us, riding back and forth fighting off the enemy and whipping up the slower horses. As we ran, partly surrounded by the enemy and all in confusion, the girth on the saddle of Howling Wolf's wife broke and she fell off her horse with the saddle, and was left behind and taken prisoner.

One of the Utes captured her and took her up behind him on his horse.

After they had taken this prisoner the enemy stopped, and presently one of our men called out to Howling Wolf, saying, "Look, look, there is your wife! They have taken her prisoner!" Howling Wolf said, "Can that be?" and then as he looked he threw down his empty gun, calling out, "Someone pick up that gun." He drew his bow and strung it, and alone charged back on the man who had his wife. The Utes had gathered in a little group about this woman, and Howling Wolf rode straight for this crowd, shooting right and left with his arrows, when he got close to them. He ran against one man, and his horse knocked down horse and rider. He passed through the crowd up to the man who had his wife as prisoner, and shot an arrow through him, and then shot another man who tried to lead off the horse the woman was riding. A third ran up to take the bridle and he shot an arrow through his head. Then all the Utes made a rush at Howling Wolf and his wife. Their horses were separated, and the woman pushed off to one side. All the Utes were shooting at Howling Wolf, and he fought until all his arrows were gone, and then he was pushed off further, and rode to us. We never knew how many of the Utes were wounded. Howling Wolf was not hurt, but his horse was shot through the mane with an arrow.

Long afterwards, we were told that the Utes said to this woman, "Who is that man who is doing all this fighting?" She answered proudly, "That man is my husband." When she said that the Utes rushed upon her and shot her with arrows, so that she died.

The enemy did not follow us further. They had killed two more of our men and this woman, and had captured all the horses we were driving. Perhaps they were satisfied.

For the last year I had been thinking a great deal about Standing Alone. I saw and spoke to her sometimes, but in these later days not so often as when I had been younger and had not been so often going on the warpath against my enemies. Yet she knew how I felt and her family and my mother also knew how I felt. She was wearing a ring of horn that I had given her and I wore her ring.

Three times in the last two years when I had come back from my war journeys with horses I had driven the horses to Two Bulls' lodge and left them there, and had sent him a message telling him that those horses were his. I had not given any present to Standing Alone.

In summer of this year I spoke to my uncle and told him that I wished to send horses to Two Bulls, and to ask him to give me his daughter for my wife. My uncle felt that this would be good and advised me to do it, saying that if I had not so many horses as I wished to send I should go to his band and take any that I liked. I told him that this need not be done for I, myself, could furnish the horses. Besides, my relations would give such other presents as might be needed.

So it happened that about the time the leaves of the cottonwoods began to turn yellow, my aunt, my mother's oldest sister, went to Two Bulls' lodge taking ten horses, which she tied before the lodge, and then, entering, gave the message, saying that Wikis wished Standing Alone for his wife. After she had said this, my aunt returned to her lodge.

That night Two Bulls sent for his relations and told them what I had said. They counseled together and agreed that the young woman should be given to me. When I learned this my heart was stirred.

The news came to my lodge through one of the women of Two Bulls' family, and my mother and sisters prepared our lodge for the coming of Standing Alone.

It was about the middle of the day when they told me that she was coming.

Standing Alone, finely dressed, was riding a handsome spotted horse led by one of her relations, and other women were coming behind, leading other horses which bore loads.

The horse ridden by Standing Alone was led up close to the lodge and my mother ran out to it. Standing Alone put her arms around my mother's neck and slipped out of the saddle on my mother's back. My sisters caught her feet and supported Standing Alone, who was thus carried on my mother's back into the lodge and her feet did not touch the ground. Then she was carried around to the back of the lodge where my sleeping place was and seated next to me on my bed. Presently food was prepared and

112

for the dish to be offered to Standing Alone my mother cut up the meat into small pieces, so that she should have no trouble in eating her food. Then Standing Alone and I ate together and so I took her for my wife.

Many of the gifts that Two Bulls had sent with Standing Alone were distributed among my relations.

That day all my near relations came, bringing gifts of many sorts to us who were newly married. They brought us a lodge and much lodge furniture—robes and bedding, backrests, mats and dishes—all the things that people used in the life of the camp. Of these presents some were sent to the relations of Standing Alone and they in turn sent other presents to us, so that as husband and wife Standing Alone and I began our life well provided with all that we needed.

I did not again go to war that year, but spent much of my time hunting—providing food for my own family and often leaving meat at my father-in-law's lodge.

Up to this time, as I look back on it to-day, it seems to me that life had been easy for me and for the tribe. We had many skins for robes, lodges and clothing. Food was plenty. If we needed horses we made journeys to war against our enemies to the south and took what we required—but hard times were coming.

It was but a few years after I took Standing Alone for my wife, when my oldest boy was four years old, that the wars were begun between the white people and my tribe.

This was a hard time. It is true we killed many white

113

people and captured much property, but though most of the tribe did not seem to see that it was so, my uncle and I felt that the Indians were being crowded out, pushed further and further away from where we had always been—where we belonged. After each expedition through the country by white troops and after each fight that we had with the white men, we felt as if some great hand that was all around my tribe and all the other tribes, was closing a little tighter about us all, and that at last it would grasp us and squeeze us to death.

Of that bad time and of what followed that time, I do not wish to speak, and so my story ends.

UNIVERSITY OF OKLAHOMA PRESS : NORMAN

DATE DUE

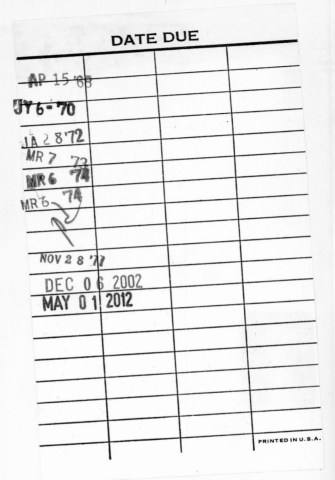